Techniques and Materials of Tonal Music

Techniques and Materials of Tonal Music

With an Introduction to Twentieth-Century Techniques

Fourth Edition

Thomas Benjamin

Peabody Conservatory
The Johns Hopkins University

Michael Horvit

School of Music
The University of Houston

Robert Nelson

School of Music
The University of Houston

Wadsworth Publishing Company
Belmont, California
A Division of Wadsworth, Inc.

Music Editor: Suzanna Brabant
Editorial Assistant: Dana Lipsky
Print Buyer: Martha Branch
Production: Greg Hubit Bookworks
Cover: Harry Voigt

Printed in the United States of America

2 3 4 5 6 7 8 9 10—96 95 94 93 92

 This book is printed on acid-free paper that meets Environmental Protection Agency standards for recycled paper.

Library of Congress Cataloging-in-Publication Data

Benjamin, Thomas.
    Techniques and materials of tonal music: with an introduction to twentieth-century techniques / Thomas Benjamin, Michael Horvit, Robert Nelson. — 4th ed.
        p. cm.
    Includes bibliographical references (p. 277) and index.
    ISBN 0-534-16680-6
    1. Music—Theory. 2. Composition (Music) I. Horvit, Michael M.
II. Nelson, Robert, 1941–   . III. Title.
MT6.B3335T4 1992
781.2—dc20
                                                        91-24504
                                                        CIP
                                                        MN

To our wives, friends, colleagues, and students

Contents

Part IV   Twentieth-Century Materials

Part V   Reference Materials

Preface

Techniques and Materials of Tonal Music, Fourth Edition, is intended to be used as a text for the first two years of college theory courses, not including ear training and sight-singing. The subject matter includes a study of the rudiments of musical materials; the harmonic, melodic, rhythmic, and basic formal procedures of the common practice period; and an introduction to the compositional techniques developed during the twentieth century. *Entering students without strong backgrounds might need to spend the first month or so using a separate fundamentals workbook.*

This book fills a need that standard theory textbooks do not satisfy. Many texts present their material in an elaborate prose format that locks the teacher into the author's method of presentation down to the smallest details. This allows for very little creativity and flexibility in the classroom. It often results in the unimaginative and educationally unproductive procedure of reading the text in class together with the students, underlining or outlining the text to distill its essentials, or ignoring the text as peripheral to the course. Many theory teachers who know their material well use no text at all because of these drawbacks.

Techniques and Materials of Tonal Music is a complete common practice theory text that also covers contemporary materials. It presents its subject matter in concise outline form, enabling the teacher to flesh out the course in a personal manner. It allows for flexibility and creativity on the part of the teacher, which leads to more direct communication and interaction between student and teacher. Students are presented with what they need to know in an accessible format.

This text grew out of our classroom experiences at the University of Houston and the institutions with which we were previously connected. The result of extensive classroom testing, it originated as a series of mimeographed handouts that were gradually refined and reorganized until they coalesced into their current form. It embodies our belief that directness and leanness of approach are desirable, as well as a firm conviction that the focus of any music course should be *on the music itself.* Toward this end, the book is intended to be used with a well-organized anthology of musical examples, such as our *Music for Analysis.* This allows the student to see the larger context in which the material under study occurs and to see it used in a variety of styles and textures.

The material is organized in outline form. In each unit a general procedure is followed: the material of the unit is described as clearly as possible, and skeletal examples of the procedures under consideration, in both keyboard and choral voicings, are interwoven with the explanatory material. The teacher and the students are continually urged to refer to the anthologies to analyze music that employs the techniques under discussion (this is essential to the approach of this book). The book contains several types of exercises. There are melodies and figured and unfigured basses for harmonization. Every effort has been made to ensure that these are as musical as possible and that the cumulative level of these examples reflects and is relevant to the level of the students' development. Further, there are exercises of a more creative, compositional nature, such as filling out or composing small forms, and exercises dealing with instrumental textures, both keyboard and chamber combinations (intended to be performed in class by the students).

An essential feature of the book is Part V, which presents summaries of several important topics. Most of this material is developed in a gradual fashion throughout the text as appropriate to each of the units. Here, however, the student can find in one place a summary of such topics as doubling, voice leading, chord-choice criteria, and so forth. Throughout the text the student is directed to Part V for such topics as textures, formal structures, and analytical procedures, to name only a few.

The approach is eclectic rather than idiosyncratic. The terminology is standard: that in general use in the United States today. Where more than one term is commonly in use, the alternate term is also given. Relevance to actual musical practice has been our primary concern. That is why we require the use of an anthology: the student should have in hand a maximum amount of music literature from which to learn.

We wish to thank the following persons, whose comments helped us in planning the Fourth Edition of *Techniques and Materials of Tonal Music*: Richard Anderson, Brigham Young University; Joyce A. Ghormley, San Jacinto College; Lewis Nielson, University of Georgia.

T. B.
M. H.
R. N.

Suggestions to the Teacher

The following comments reflect the way in which we have used this book and are intended only to be general guidelines.

1. Analysis

Many examples from the literature, with as broad a stylistic scope as possible, must be used in presenting the material of each unit; all examples must be played in class. For this reason we recommend the adoption of a supplementary music anthology. Our *Music for Analysis* contains excerpts and complete pieces from the common practice period and the twentieth century and is organized for use with this book. Several other suitable anthologies are listed in the Bibliography.

The instructor should go beyond mere harmonic analysis in discussion. Constant reference should be made in analysis and in criticism of student writing to such important matters as motivic unity, melodic construction, counterpoint, cadence and phrase structure, harmonic rhythm, and any special features of a given work. For a more complete listing of elements, see the Checklist for Analysis, Part V, Unit 21.

Stylistic and historical aspects of the music are in a sense incidental in analysis, but they may be considered to give an extra dimension to the discussion. Problems of performance as they are clarified by analysis often interest students.

In class discussion, the instructor should emphasize the organic nature of music—that is, the interactions of line, rhythm, harmony, and so on. It may be pedagogically useful to treat all elements separately at first, but the unifying aspects should be brought out as early as possible. Complete short works should be studied periodically to show large-scale applications of various materials and techniques.

For analysis, the instructor should choose music that exhibits a wide variety of textures, instrumental idioms, and harmonic rhythms, as well as avoid overdependence on the four-voice chorale style.

2. Reference materials

Continual use of the reference section (Part V) for summaries and detailed explanations is urged. Most of the topics covered in it are broadly applicable throughout the text. Of particular interest are the units dealing with form (Units 13, 14, and 20).

3. Written work

Statements regarding doubling and voice leading within Parts II and III apply to strict four-part writing. Obviously, the musical examples will exhibit a wider variety of procedures as a result of the textures and idioms employed. There are more exercises in each unit than most instructors will find practical to use. These exercises range from basic part-writing work to exercises in various textures and styles. It is hoped that the instructor will make use of a wide spectrum of exercises.

In the creative writing exercises, the instructor should make use of the various instruments and voices available in class. He or she should discuss all instruments to be used and refer to the information on instrument ranges found in Part V, Unit 23.

All student writing in which there is any degree of creativity should be played in class and discussed. Musicality, as well as technical competence, should be emphasized.

4. Keyboard applications

Keyboard application of all basic material in this text is strongly recommended. Any of the available keyboard harmony textbooks may be used.

5. Sight-singing and ear training

It is assumed that sight-singing drill is an integral part of the theory program. We suggest doing as much part-singing as possible. Several good collections of music for singing, such as the author's *Music for Sight-Singing* (Houghton Mifflin, 1984), are available.

Both sight-singing and ear-training work should be coordinated with the theory course. The instructor should stress the importance of listening to both written and analytical assignments before students hand them in.

6. Improvisation

Three types of exercises in this book lend themselves to classroom improvisation: melodies for harmonization, figured-bass exercises, and phrase-chord formats. These may be done with piano alone, piano plus instruments, or groups of instruments without piano.

7. Rudiments of music

Part I is intended as a review of musical fundamentals. When dealing with a class whose background in rudiments is not strong, the instructor may wish to use one of the many available programmed fundamentals workbooks as a supplement. See the Bibliography.

8. Analytical symbols

The analytical system used throughout employs roman numerals to indicate chord function and quality, together with traditional figured-bass symbols that show inversion, precise interval structure, and chromatic alterations. The instructor may of course use any modification of this sytem desired.

Techniques and Materials of Tonal Music

Part I

Rudiments

1 The Great Staff and Piano Keyboard

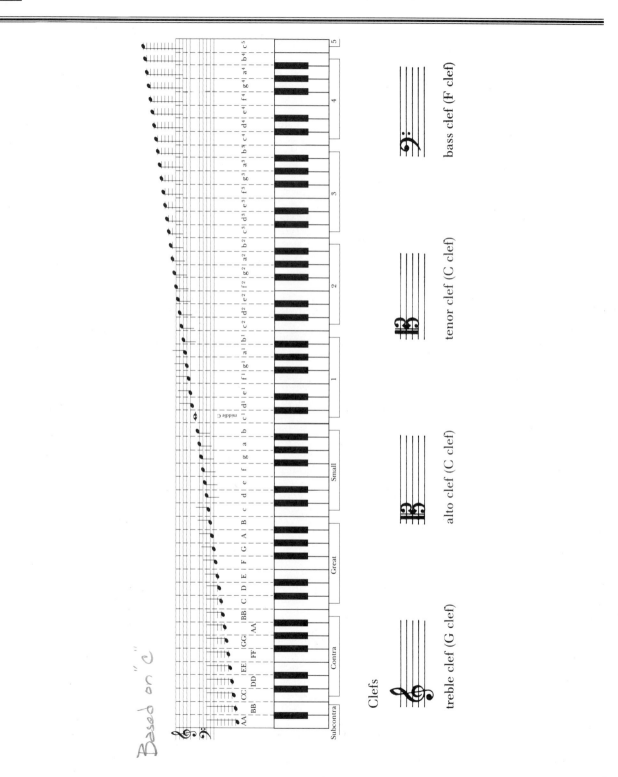

Based on "C"

Clefs

treble clef (G clef)

alto clef (C clef)

tenor clef (C clef)

bass clef (F clef)

2 Accidentals

I. An *accidental* is a sign at the left of a musical note that indicates a change in the note's pitch.

A. ♯ A *sharp* raises the pitch of a note one half step above its natural pitch.

 = one half step higher than

B. × A *double sharp* raises the pitch of a note two half steps above its natural pitch.

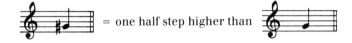 = two half steps higher than

C. ♭ A *flat* lowers the pitch of a note one half step below its natural pitch.

 = one half step below

D. ♭♭ A *double flat* lowers the pitch of a note two half steps below its natural pitch.

 = two half steps below

E. ♮ A *natural* cancels an accidental previously in effect.

*This pitch is G natural.

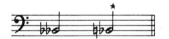

*This pitch is B flat.

*This pitch is F natural.

II. If a note has been altered by either a key signature (see Part I, Unit 5) or a previous accidental, a *double accidental* is used to further alter the note one half step.

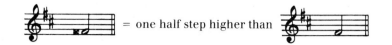

III. Accidentals are often carelessly written, even in some printed music. The following observations on the proper use of accidentals in tonal music should be carefully noted.

   A. Accidentals do not carry into other octaves in the same measure; one should specify the desired accidental.

   B. Though a bar-line technically cancels an accidental from the preceding measure, one should specify the desired accidental in the new measure, in parentheses.

   C. If there is an accidental early in a measure, it is wise to restate it parenthetically later in the same measure.

3 Intervals

Read
for
14 Sept.

I. An *interval* is the distance between two pitches.

    A. This distance is measured by the number of whole and/or half steps it contains.

    B. The names for intervals correspond to the number of different names of notes the interval contains.
        1. The distance from C to E is a third (contains three note names: C, D, and E).
        2. The distance from C to B is a seventh (contains seven note names: C, D, E, F, G, A, and B).
        3. The size of an interval is indicated by an arabic numeral (for example, third = 3).

    C. Intervals are classified as major (M), minor (m), perfect (P), diminished (d), and augmented (A).
        1. 1, 4, 5, and 8 may be only P, d, or A.
        2. 2, 3, 6, and 7 may be only M, m, d, or A.

II. The following intervals are contained within the span of an octave:

P1, or perfect unison (prime) = 2 notes on same pitch

m2, or minor second = ½ step

M2, or major second = 1 step

m3, or minor third = 1½ steps (M2 + m2)

M3, or major third = 2 steps (M2 + M2)

P4, or perfect fourth = 2½ steps (M3 + m2)

A4, or augmented fourth = 3 steps (M3 + M2)*   } Tri-tone

d5, or diminished fifth = 3 steps (P4 + m2)*

P5, or perfect fifth = 3½ steps (M3 + m3; or P4 + M2)

m6, or minor sixth = 4 steps (P5 + m2)

M6, or major sixth = 4½ steps (P5 + M2)

m7, or minor seventh = 5 steps (P5 + m3)

M7, or major seventh = 5½ steps (P5 + M3)

P8, or perfect octave = 6 steps (P5 + P4)

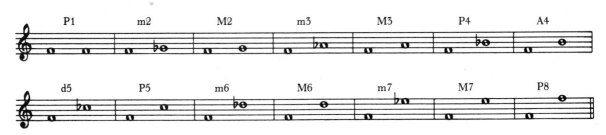

---

*See enharmonic intervals, IV.

III. Relationships of interval classifications.

    A. Major intervals are one half step larger than minor intervals.

    B. Augmented intervals are one half step larger than perfect or major intervals.

    C. Diminished intervals are one half step smaller than perfect or minor intervals.

IV. Intervals that sound the same pitches but are spelled differently and thus function differently are called *enharmonic intervals.*

V. The d5 and A4 are enharmonic intervals (see IV-B for an example). Both these intervals contain three whole steps (tones), and both are commonly referred to as the *tritone (T) intervals.*

VI. Intervals that are larger than an octave are referred to as *compound intervals.*

    A. P8 + M2 = M9

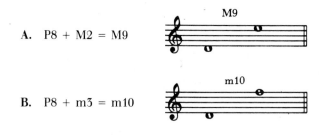

    B. P8 + m3 = m10

VII. Inversion of intervals.

    A. An interval is inverted by transferring its lower note into the higher octave or by transferring its higher note into the lower octave.

    B. Major intervals invert to minor intervals, and minor intervals invert to major intervals.

        1. m2 inverts to M7, and M7 inverts to m2.

2. M2 inverts to m7, and m7 inverts to M2.

3. m3 inverts to M6, and M6 inverts to m3.

4. M3 inverts to m6, and m6 inverts to M3.

C. Perfect intervals invert to perfect intervals.

D. Augmented intervals invert to diminished intervals, and diminished intervals invert to augmented intervals.
    1. d5 inverts to A4, and A4 inverts to d5.

    2. A6 inverts to d3, and d3 inverts to A6.

    3. d7 inverts to A2, and A2 inverts to d7.

VII. A *harmonic interval* is one in which the pitches are sounded simultaneously.

IX. A *melodic interval* is one in which the pitches are sounded consecutively.

X. Note that when the same accidental is applied to both notes of an interval, the size remains the same.

XI. In tonal music, intervals are classified as either *consonant* (stable) or *dissonant* (unstable).*

    A. Consonances
        1. Perfect consonances include P1, P5, P8, and P4 (depending upon the context).
        2. Imperfect consonances include m3, M3, m6, and M6.

    B. Dissonances include m2, M2, m7, M7; all augmented and diminished intervals; and P4 (depending upon the context).

XII. A summary of all the diatonic intervals found within the major and minor scales will be found in the next unit.

Exercises

1. Identify the following intervals:

    a.

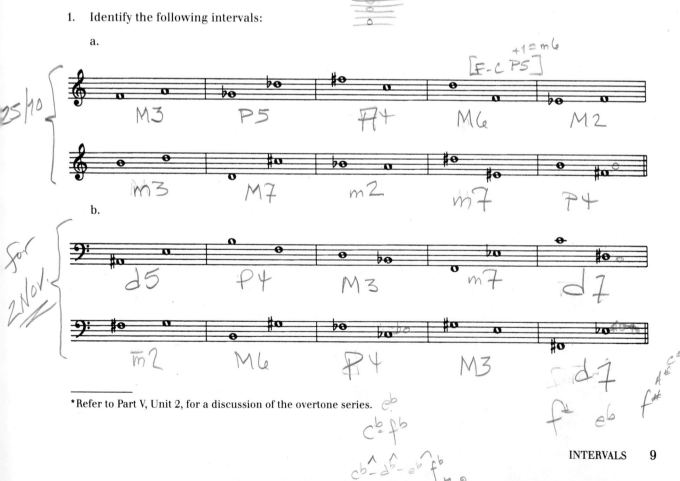

    b.

---

*Refer to Part V, Unit 2, for a discussion of the overtone series.

2. Write the notes that form the indicated intervals above the given pitch.

a.

b.

c.

d.

e.

3. Write the notes that form the indicated intervals below the given pitch.

a.

b.

c.

d.

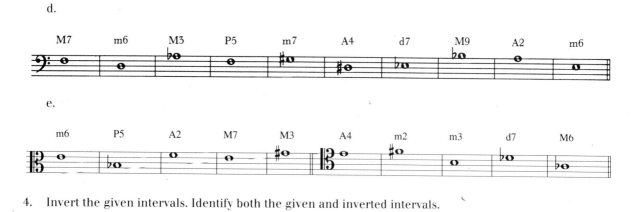

e.

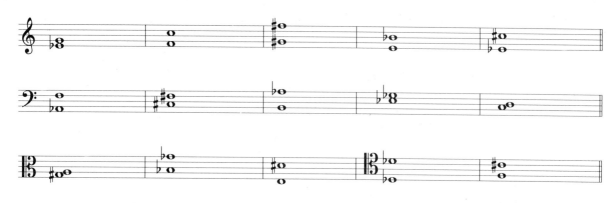

4. Invert the given intervals. Identify both the given and inverted intervals.

5. Name the bracketed intervals in the following melodies:

    a.   Symphony No. 4, first movement   Brahms

b.   *Tristan und Isolde*, Act 3

4 Major and Minor Scales

I. The following succession of intervals, demonstrated with the C-major scale, is needed to construct a *major scale* above any given tonic (key-note). The following symbols are used to indicate the size of the steps (seconds) between successive notes: ∧ denotes a major second, and ⌢ denotes a minor second.

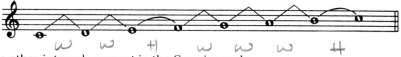

Following are the other intervals present in the C-major scale.

A. Sevenths.

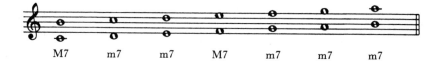

M7   m7   m7   M7   m7   m7   m7

B. Thirds and sixths.

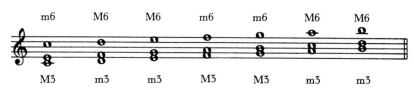

C. Fourths and fifths.

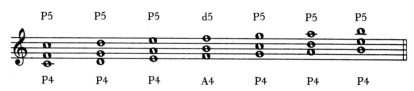

II. *Minor scales* have three traditional theoretical forms—natural (pure), harmonic, and melodic—shown here with the A-minor scale. There is rarely a clear distinction between these forms in actual music. Context alone determines which forms of the variable sixth and seventh scale-degrees will be used in a given passage. In the following chart, the symbol ⌐ is used to indicate the augmented second:

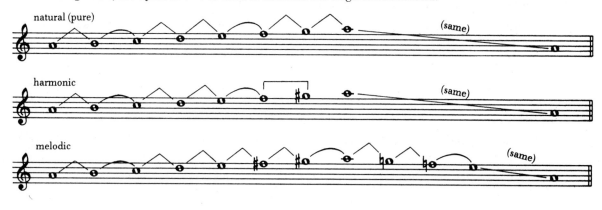

In all minor scale-forms, scale-degrees one through five are invariable. The natural and harmonic forms are the same ascending and descending, whereas the melodic form is variable. All alterations are to the sixth and seventh degrees. The descending form of the melodic minor is the same as the natural minor.

Following are the other intervals present in the C-natural minor scale.

A. Sevenths.

B. Thirds and sixths.

C. Fourths and fifths.

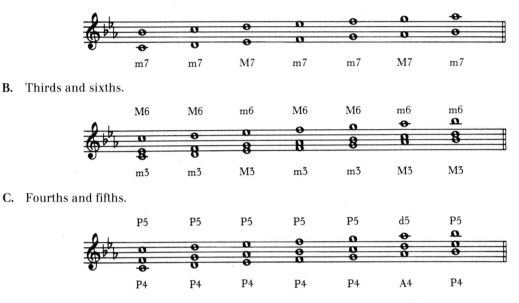

III. Scale-degree names:

1 is the tonic.	5 is the dominant.
2 is the supertonic.	6 is the submediant.
3 is the mediant.	7 is the subtonic (when an M2 below tonic).
4 is the subdominant.	7 is the leading tone (when an m2 below tonic).

Exercises

1. Write the following major scales up one octave from tonic to tonic, using the treble staff: G, F, A, Eb, B, Db. Use accidentals as they are required to form the proper interval series. Do not use key signatures.

2. Write the following major scales according to the instructions for Exercise 1, using the bass staff: D, Bb, E, Ab, F♯, Gb.

3. Write the following major scales according to the instructions for Exercise 1, using the alto clef: G, Bb, A.

4. Write the following major scales, using the tenor clef: F, D, Eb.

5. Write the following minor scales, according to the instructions for Exercise 1, in both treble and bass staves:

Natural	Harmonic	Melodic
eb	d	eb
a	bb	g♯
b	c♯	e

The natural and harmonic forms may be written only ascending; the melodic form must be written both ascending and descending.

6. Write the following minor scales as above, using both alto and tenor clefs: ab, b, c.

5 Key Signatures

I. *Key signatures* arise from the need for certain consistent accidentals within keys (that is, to secure the desired scale-form above a given tonic). Here is the D-major scale and key signature:

II. Each major key has a *relative minor* whose tonic is on the sixth scale-degree of the major (and a minor third below the tonic) and that uses the same key signature. Large letters are used to stand for major keys and small letters, for minor keys; thus e is the relative of G.

III. Parallel major and minor keys have the same tonic; thus F major is the parallel of F minor. *Parallel keys* have signatures that differ by three accidentals.

F major   F minor

IV. Charts of key signatures.

A. For the "sharp" keys, successive tonics are related by ascending perfect fifths.

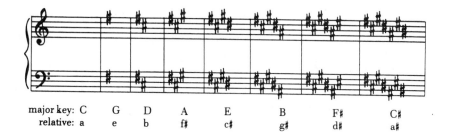

major key:	C	G	D	A	E	B	F♯	C♯
relative:	a	e	b	f♯	c♯	g♯	d♯	a♯

B. For the "flat" keys, successive tonics are related by descending perfect fifths.

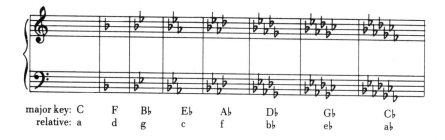

major key:	C	F	B♭	E♭	A♭	D♭	G♭	C♭
relative:	a	d	g	c	f	b♭	e♭	a♭

V. The order in which key signatures are written on the staff is given as follows. Sharps are read from left to right and flats, from right to left.

$\sharp \longrightarrow$

F C G D A E B

$\longleftarrow \flat$

VI. The *circle of fifths* is a traditional graphic arrangement that shows the major and minor keys with their key signatures.

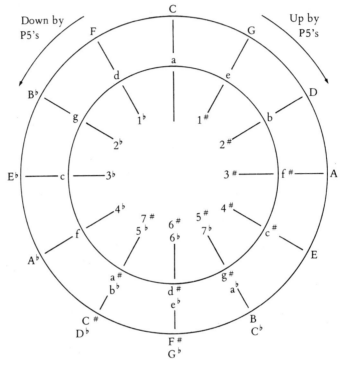

Exercises

1. Using the great staff, write the following key signatures: D, B♭, A, E♭, B, D♭, g, b, c, f, f♯, e.

2. Give the relative and parallel keys for the following keys: C, E, a, d, g♯, c♯, E♭, C♯.

3. Using key signatures and accidentals as needed, write the following minor scales in both staves of the great staff:

Natural	Harmonic	Melodic
b	e	c
c♯	b♭	f♯
f	g♯	g
d	e♭	a♭

Using key signatures and accidentals as needed, write the following minor scales in both the alto and tenor clefs.

Natural	Harmonic	Melodic
g♯	c♯	a♯
b♭	g	d
c	e	e♭
f♯	f	b

6 Meter and Rhythm

I. Note value and rests.

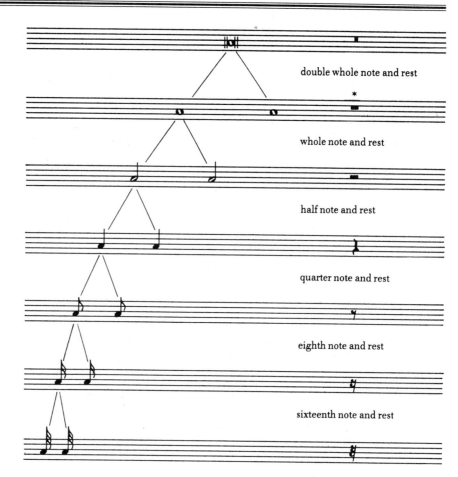

double whole note and rest

whole note and rest*

half note and rest

quarter note and rest

eighth note and rest

sixteenth note and rest

thirty-second note and rest

A. Dots add half the value of the note; a second dot adds half the value of the first dot.

*A whole rest is often used to indicate the total duration of a measure regardless of the meter.

17

B. Other durations may be achieved by use of the tie. The tie must be used for durations extending from one measure to another.

II. *Meter* is the organization of musical time into recurring patterns of accent (stress). Each complete pattern constitutes a *measure*, and the measures are divided by *bar lines*. The particular pattern is indicated by a *meter signature (time signature)*. The first beat of every measure is called the *downbeat*.

Common Metric Patterns

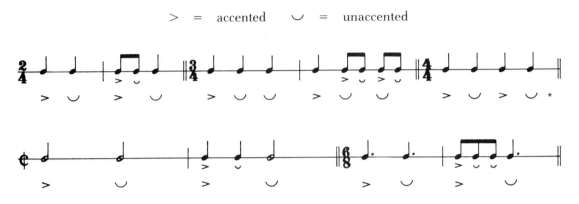

Note that a similar alternation of accent and unaccent is found in the division of the beat.

Meter Signatures

		Simple		Compound	
Duple	(beat unit)	$\frac{2}{2}$ ¢		$\frac{6}{4}$	
	(background unit)				
		$\frac{2}{4}$		$\frac{6}{8}$	
		$\frac{2}{8}$		$\frac{6}{16}$	

---

*In earlier common practice styles no distinction is made between the first and third beats. However, in later styles the two are differentiated; the first beat becomes a primary accent and the third beat, a secondary accent.

	Simple		Compound	
Triple	$\frac{3}{2}$	(notation)	$\frac{9}{4}$	(notation)
	$\frac{3}{4}$	(notation)	$\frac{9}{8}$	(notation)
	$\frac{3}{8}$	(notation)	$\frac{9}{16}$	(notation)
Quadruple	$\frac{4}{2}$	(notation)	$\frac{12}{4}$	(notation)
	$\frac{4}{4}$ C	(notation)	$\frac{12}{8}$	(notation)
	$\frac{4}{8}$	(notation)	$\frac{12}{16}$	(notation)

A. Meters are classified according to the number of background units and the number of beats per measure. The *background unit* is the note value representing the largest possible division of the beat unit as shown in the table above. *Simple meters* have two background units per beat; *compound meters* have three background units per beat. (Note that consequently the beat units of compound meters are always dotted notes.) Meters having two beats per bar are *duple*; three beats per bar, *triple*; four beats per bar, *quadruple*; and five beats per bar, *quintuple.**

In simple meters the upper number of the time signature indicates the number of beats, and the lower number indicates the note value of the beat. In compound meters the upper number indicates the number of background units and the lower number, the value of the background unit. To find the number of beats in compound meter, divide the upper number by 3.

The meter signature is placed after the key signature on the first system and is not repeated on subsequent systems.

---

*Quintuple meter is often termed a *composite meter*, as it can be considered a combination of duple and triple meters. See Part IV, Unit 3.

B. *Related meters* are meters having the same number of beats and the same type of division of the beat (either simple or compound) but different beat values, for example, $\frac{2}{4}$ and $\frac{2}{8}$. (Refer to the table on meter signatures.)

C. *Equivalent meters* are meters having the same number of beats and the same background unit but different divisions of the beat. For example, $\frac{2}{4}$ and $\frac{6}{8}$ both have two beats per measure and a background unit of the eighth note. However, $\frac{2}{4}$ has two eighth notes per beat, whereas $\frac{6}{8}$ has three eighth notes per beat. Divisions in compound meter can be expressed in simple meter by use of the triplet figure; simple into compound, by use of the duplet.

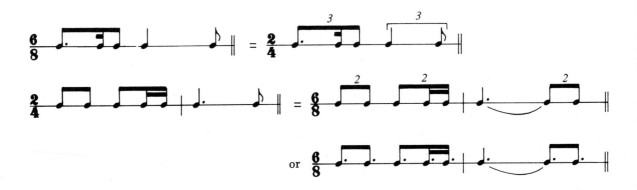

III. *Rhythm* generally refers to the actual choice and distribution of notes within a bar. Beyond the need to have the total value of the notes equal the value indicated by the meter signature, certain notational conventions should be considered. Groups of notes with flags are generally connected by *beams*.

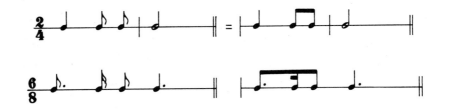

These groupings should reflect the meter.

Beams are preferable to single stems and flags except in vocal music, which traditionally gives each syllable a separate note.

IV. Establishment of meter.

A. *Agogic accent* is the use of relatively longer note values to establish meter.

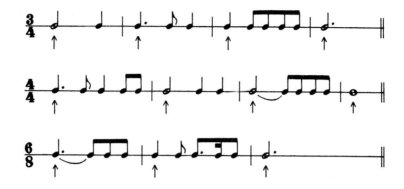

B. *Melodic pitch patterns* establish accent through melodic patterning.

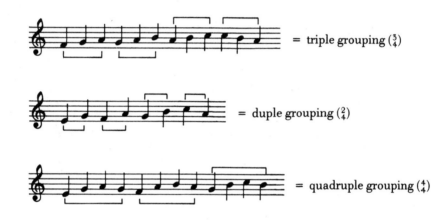

= triple grouping ($\frac{3}{4}$)

= duple grouping ($\frac{2}{4}$)

= quadruple grouping ($\frac{4}{4}$)

C. *Accompanimental patterns* may establish metric accent by bass note placement and establish weak beats or parts of beats by chord or inner-voice placement.

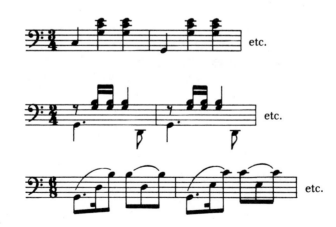

D. *Metric stress* may be established by accent marks or dynamics.

etc.

etc.

V. *Syncopation* is the displacement of accent in which accented notes occur on normally unaccented beats or parts of beats. This displacement can be affected by any of the four devices of establishing meter just described.

   A. Agogic accent.

B. Melodic pitch patterns.

C. Accompanimental patterns.

D. Artificial accent.

Exercises

1. Identify the following meter signatures by indicating the number of beats, the note value receiving one beat, the division of the beat, and the terminology for the meter:

Meter	Beats	Unit of Beat	Background Unit	Terminology
2/4	two	♩ (quarter note)	♪ (eighth note)	simple duple
3/4				
6/8				
4/4				
C				
2/2				
6/4				
3/8				

a. Complete the chart below:

Meter	Beats	Unit of Beat	Background Unit	Terminology
2/4				
				compound duple
¢				
			♪ (eighth note)	simple _____
	3/4	𝅗𝅥 (half note)		simple _____
9/8				
	2	𝅘𝅥. (dotted quarter note)		
			♩ (quarter note)	compound triple

2. Give the equivalent number of indicated values for the note shown.

Example: ♩ = 2 eighth notes

    a.   Undotted note values:

𝅝 _____ half notes   ♩ _____ thirty-second notes

𝅝 _____ quarter notes   ♩ _____ eighth notes

𝅝 _____ eighth notes   ♩ _____ sixteenth notes

𝅝 _____ sixteenth notes   ♩ _____ thirty-second notes

𝅗𝅥 _____ quarter notes   ♪ _____ sixteenth notes

𝅗𝅥 _____ eighth notes   ♪ _____ thirty-second notes

𝅗𝅥 _____ sixteenth notes   𝅘𝅥𝅯 _____ thirty-second notes

    b.   Dotted note values:

𝅝· _____ half notes   ♩· _____ thirty-second notes

𝅝· _____ quarter notes   ♩· _____ sixty-fourth notes

𝅝· _____ eighth notes   ♪· _____ sixteenth notes

𝅗𝅥· _____ quarter notes   ♪· _____ thirty-second notes

𝅗𝅥· _____ eighth notes   ♪· _____ sixty-fourth notes

𝅗𝅥· _____ sixteenth notes   𝅘𝅥𝅯· _____ thirty-second notes

♩· _____ eighth notes   𝅘𝅥𝅯· _____ sixty-fourth notes

♩· _____ sixteenth notes   𝅘𝅥𝅰· _____ sixty-fourth notes

    c.   Tied note values:

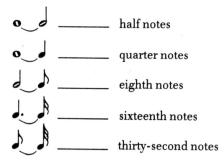

𝅝‿𝅗𝅥 _____ half notes

𝅝‿𝅗𝅥 _____ quarter notes

𝅗𝅥‿♪ _____ eighth notes

♩·‿♪ _____ sixteenth notes

♪‿𝅘𝅥𝅯 _____ thirty-second notes

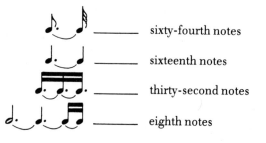

♪·‿𝅘𝅥𝅰 _____ sixty-fourth notes

♩·‿𝅗𝅥 _____ sixteenth notes

♩·‿♩·‿♩· _____ thirty-second notes

𝅗𝅥·‿♩·‿𝅘𝅥𝅯 _____ eighth notes

3. The following examples are given ungrouped and without measure bars. Add measure bars, and group eighth notes and smaller values with beams as they would normally appear in the given meter. The first note is always a downbeat.

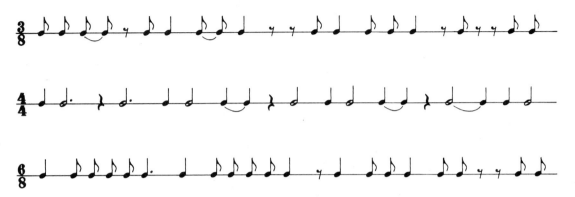

4. What meter signature does each of the following patterns suggest? Examine the patterns, determine the meter signature of each, add this signature at the beginning of the example, and draw in measure bars. Each example will be *four* full measures.

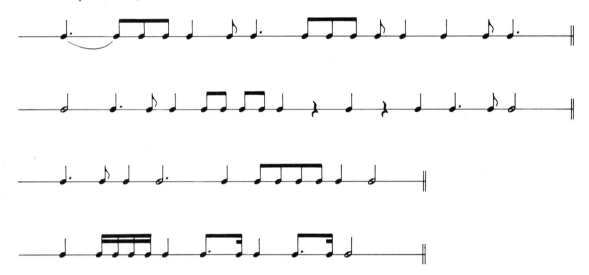

5. In the following examples replace the ties with dotted notes wherever possible. The duration of each note should remain the same.

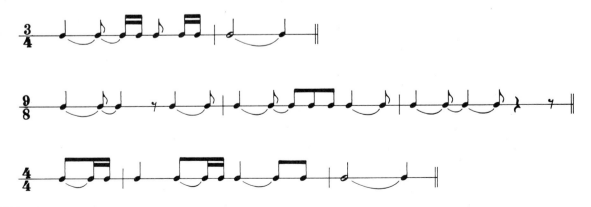

6. Notate the following examples in the related meters indicated. In other words, keep the same number of notes in each measure and the same rhythmic relationships, only changing the note values to fit the meter.

Example

Rewrite the following in $\frac{2}{8}$ and $\frac{2}{2}$:

Rewrite the following in $\frac{4}{8}$ and $\frac{4}{2}$.

Rewrite the following in $\frac{6}{16}$ and $\frac{6}{4}$.

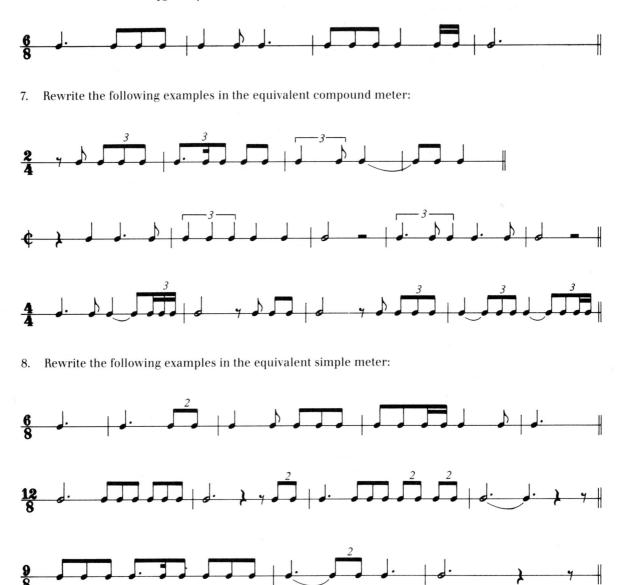

7.   Rewrite the following examples in the equivalent compound meter:

8.   Rewrite the following examples in the equivalent simple meter:

Part **II**

Diatonic Materials

↳ within the scale/key

1 Triads in Root Position

I. A *triad* is a three-tone chord consisting of superimposed thirds. The lowest note is called the *root*; the middle note is called the *third*; and the uppermost note is called the *fifth*.

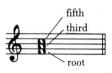

A. A *major triad* has the following intervallic structure: M3 between root and third, m3 between third and fifth, and P5 between root and fifth.

B. A *minor triad* has the following intervallic structure: m3 between root and third, M3 between third and fifth, and P5 between root and fifth.

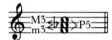

C. An *augmented triad* has the following intervallic structure: M3 between root and third, M3 between third and fifth, and A5 between root and fifth.

D. A *diminished triad* has the following intervallic structure: m3 between root and third, m3 between third and fifth, and d5 between root and fifth.

II. A triad is in *root position* if the root is in the bass. A triad takes its name from its root and its structure of interval relationships. Thus the example in I–A is an F-major triad; the example in I–B is an F-minor triad; the example in I–C is an F-augmented triad; and the example in I–D is an F-diminished triad.

Distinguish ROOT from BASS

III. Voicing.

  A. In keyboard voicing, soprano, alto, and tenor are on the upper staff; bass is on the lower staff.

  B. In choral voicing, soprano and alto are on the upper staff; tenor and bass are on the lower staff.

IV. Directions of stems.

  A. Single voice on the staff: When the note head is on or above the center line (third line) of the staff, the stem goes down; when the note head is below the center line of the staff, the stem goes up.

  B. Two voices on the staff: Stems for the upper voice go up; stems for the lower voice go down.

  C. Three voices on the staff (as in keyboard voicing): When at least two note heads lie above the center line of the staff, the stem goes down; when at least two note heads lie below the center line of the staff, the stem goes up; when the note heads lie equally above and below the center line of the staff, the stem may go in either direction.

 V. Since the triad contains three notes and four voices are to be employed, one tone must be doubled. Initially, only the root is to be doubled. (See the examples in III–A and III–B.)

VI. Spacing.

  A. In *close spacing*, the three upper voices are as close together as possible.

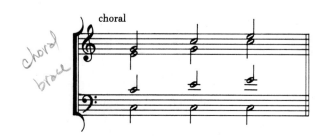

B. In *open spacing*, a tone of the same triad can be placed between each adjacent pair of upper voices (alto and tenor, soprano and alto).

C. Strict four-part exercises.
1. Avoid intervals larger than an octave between adjacent upper voices. Any interval between bass and tenor is allowed. In the *incorrect* examples that follow, note the gap between alto and tenor in the first and between soprano and alto in the second:

2. Maintain the normal order of voices. Soprano is the uppermost voice; alto is the second voice from the top, below soprano and above tenor; tenor is the second voice from the bottom, below alto and above bass; and bass is the lowest voice. In the *incorrect* example that follows, note that tenor is above alto:

D. Choral voice ranges.

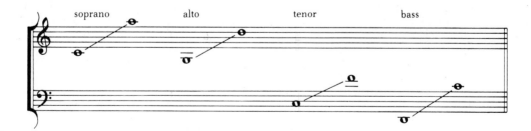

Exercises

In all written work the student should be attentive to the details of musical calligraphy. (Refer to Part V, Unit 1.)

1. Construct the following triads using three notes only on the treble staff and using accidentals as required: E major, C minor, F♯ diminished, B♭ augmented, C♯ minor, G diminished, A augmented, D♭ major, A major, E♭ minor.

2. Construct the indicated triads in the indicated voicings and spacings, using root position. Check spacing, doubling, and stem directions.

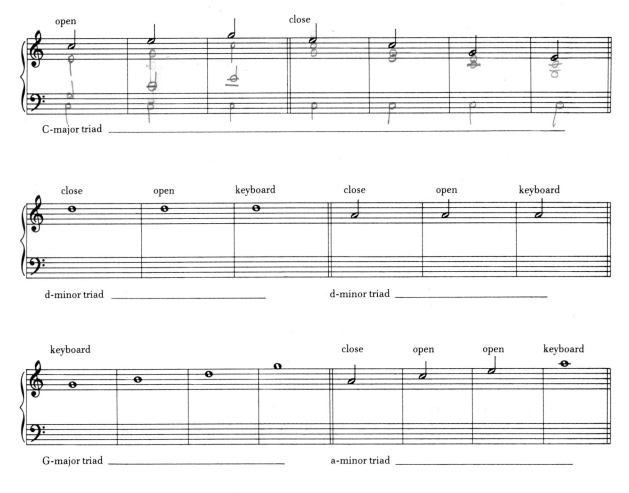

3. Construct the following triads on the great staff in root position in choral close and open spacings and keyboard voicing, using accidentals as required: D major, B♭ major, F major, A minor, A♭ major, B minor, E minor, G major, C minor, and F♯ minor. Use half notes, observing proper stem directions.

2 The Tonic Triad in Root Position

C: I   c: i

I. The roman numerals I and i refer to the major and minor triads, respectively, built on the first scale-degree *(tonic triad)*. In a major key the tonic triad is major and in a minor key the tonic triad is minor. The quality of the triad is designated by the roman numeral: uppercase for major and lowercase for minor.

II. In strict four-part writing, only the root is to be doubled at this point.

III. For voice leading in strict four-part writing, refer to Part V, Units 4 and 5, for definitions and a summary of procedures. In chord repetition, wherever possible, keep the same spacing from one chord to the next.

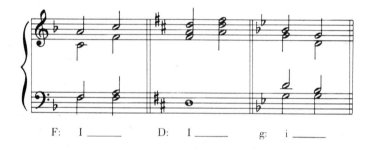

F: I _____   D: I _____   g: i _____

A. In choral voicing a change from close to open spacing or the reverse will often be preferable when an interval larger than a fourth occurs in the soprano. In keyboard voicing, however, the notes in the right hand are always kept in close position. This necessitates overlapping when there is a wide leap in the soprano.

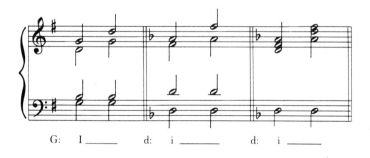

G: I _____   d: i _____   d: i _____

B. Contrary motion can often be achieved through a change of spacing.

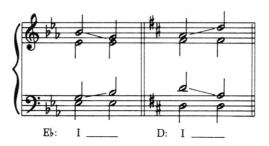

E♭: I _____   D: I _____

Students should observe that doubling and voice leading may differ from these norms, depending upon the texture of the musical example being analyzed.

Analysis

Analyze music assigned by the instructor. Refer to Part V, Units 15 and 17, and the Checklist for Analysis (Part V, Unit 21). In this and all subsequent music discussed in class, consider the following:

1. What is the texture?

2. Is the music motivically organized? If so, identify the motive or motives, and discuss the techniques of motivic development.

Exercises

1. Harmonize the following soprano lines in the indicated voicings and spacings, using the tonic triad in root position only. Check spacing, doubling, and stem direction, and play each individual voice.

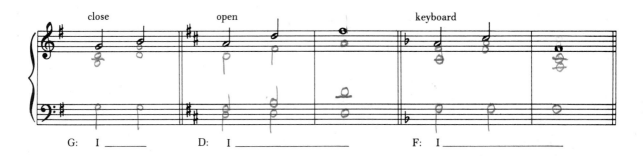

G: I _____   D: I _____   F: I _____

d: i _____   b: i _____   e: i _____

2. Harmonize the following two- and four-note sopranos in both keyboard and choral voicings, using the tonic triad in root position *only*. Close or open choral spacing will be determined by the register of the soprano. Below each example, give the roman numeral analysis of the chord. (*Note*: The given notes should appear as the highest voice [soprano], and the stem directions must be adjusted to suit the type of voicing involved.)

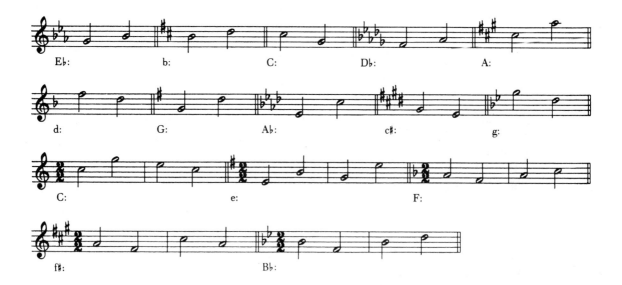

Eb: b: C: Db: A:

d: G: Ab: c#: g:

C: e: F:

f#: Bb:

3 Connection of Tonic and Dominant Triads in Root Position

C: V   c: V♮

I. The roman numeral V refers to the major triad built on the fifth degree of the scale *(dominant triad)*. In minor keys the third of the dominant triad, the *leading tone*, must be raised. The accidental that affects the leading tone is shown next to the roman numeral V.

II. The V chord may be preceded or followed by the I chord.

III. Ends of phrases are established by cadences, which articulate points of arrival or rest in the musical flow.

When the progression V–I occurs at the end of a phrase, it is termed an *authentic cadence* (A.C.). When the V chord occurs at the end of a phrase, it is termed a *half cadence* (H.C.). (See Part V, Unit 13.)

IV. At this point, only the root is to be doubled in both the I and the V triads. In any case, doubling the third of the V chord, the leading tone (a *tendency tone*, or tone that tends to move stepwise to a tone of resolution) is to be avoided.

V. There are two basic procedures for the connection of I and V in root position with the root doubled.

   A. Common tone connection.
      1. The bass takes the root of the second chord.
      2. The common tone is retained in the *same voice* in the second chord.
      3. The remaining two upper voices move by conjunct (stepwise) motion to the nearest notes of the second chord. In this connection of V to I, the leading tone normally resolves stepwise to the tonic.

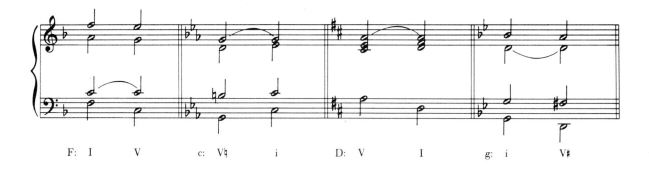

F: I   V   c: V♮   i   D: V   I   g: i   V♯

   B. Noncommon tone connection.
      1. When the soprano line involves scale-degrees 2-1, 1-2, 3-5, 5-3, or 5-7, the three upper voices normally move contrary to the bass to the nearest notes of the second chord.

d: V♯   i   A: I   V   e: V♯   i

Notice that in this connection of V to I, the leading tone, a tendency tone, does not resolve to tonic, but skips to the dominant. This is known as a *free resolution of the leading tone.* This can occur *only* when the leading tone is in an inner voice.

2. The following is an exceptional procedure to achieve change of spacing when the third of the first chord proceeds to the third of the second chord:

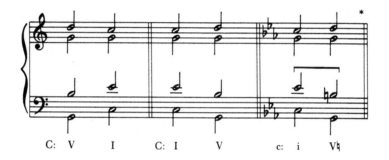

C: V   I   C: I   V   c: i   V♮

VI. See Part V, Unit 4, for definitions and examples of relative and linear motion.

VII. Any note that is not heard as a member of the prevailing harmony (chord) at any given time is defined as a *nonharmonic (nonchord) tone.* The following are two common types of nonharmonic tones; other types will be introduced in subsequent units. Nonharmonic tones may occur simultaneously in more than one voice, in which case they are usually consonant with each other. Excessive nonharmonic activity may obscure the underlying harmonic structure.

A. Passing tone (p.t.). See Part V, Unit 3, for definition.

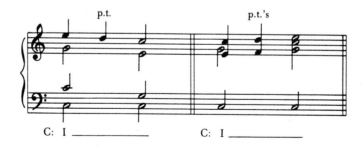

C: I _____   C: I _____

_____

*This exceptional procedure rarely occurs in minor keys, because of the diminished fourth between the thirds of the two chords.

Note the use of the ascending form of the minor scale to avoid the augmented second.

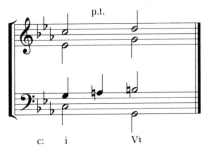

c: i   V♮

B.   Auxiliary (aux.) or neighbor tone (n.t.).

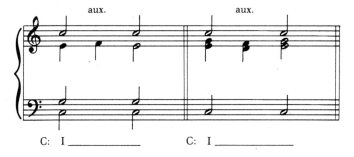

C: I _____   C: I _____

Analysis

Analyze music assigned by the instructor. Refer to Part V, Units 3 and 18, for a discussion of nonharmonic tones and melody. In this and all subsequent music discussed in class, consider the following:

1.   How are harmonies implied melodically?

2.   What is the relationship of harmonic and nonharmonic tones in the melodic line?

3.   What is the basic shape of the melodic line?

4.   How is continuity achieved?

5.   What pitches seem structurally important? Why?

Exercises

The following exercises are to be done on the great staff, employing the tonic and dominant triads in root position.

1.   Harmonize the following soprano examples, employing choral open, choral close, or keyboard voicing as indicated:

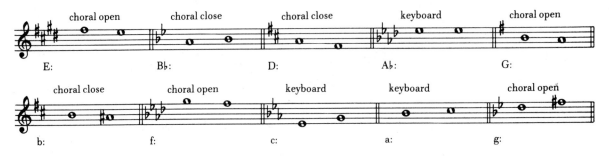

2. Harmonize the following soprano examples according to the directions for Exercise 1:

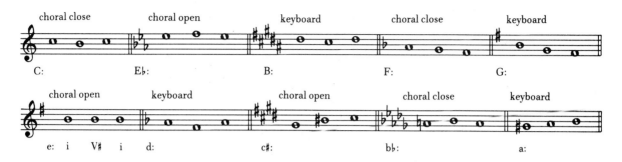

3. Introduce passing tones in the following progressions:

4. Introduce auxiliaries in the following progressions:

5. Harmonize the following soprano melodies. Passing tones and auxiliaries may be employed as directed by the instructor. Analyze the cadences. In choral voicing, open or close spacing will be dictated by the register of the soprano, unless otherwise designated by the instructor.

    a.

    b.

c.

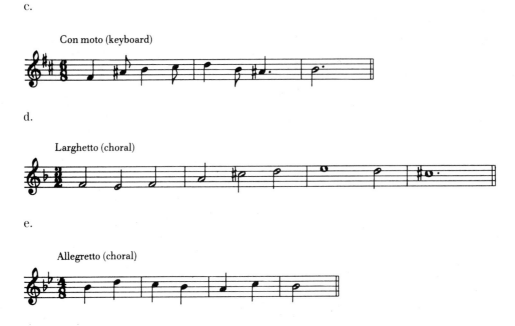

Con moto (keyboard)

d.

Larghetto (choral)

e.

Allegretto (choral)

6. The following patterns may be used for composing melodies, for practice in working with nonharmonic tones, for two voice (soprano and bass) textures, or for improvisation. Be conscious of motivic consistency, direction of line, rhythmic continuity, and clarity of cadence. Refer to Part V, Unit 18, for a discussion of melody. (Note values represent harmonic rhythm.)

    Moderato
a. F major: **3/4**   I | I | V | I   ‖

    Adagio
b. C minor: **4/4**   i   V♮ | i   V♮ | i V♮ i V♮ | i   ‖

    Con moto
c. A major: **6/8**   I   V | I   V | I   V | I   ‖

4. The Dominant Seventh Chord in Root Position

C: V7   c: V$^7_4$

1. The *dominant seventh chord* (V7) consists of a major triad with a minor seventh (Mm7); note the dissonant tritone and minor seventh. In minor keys, the third of the chord (the leading tone) must be raised.

II. The V7 functions in the same way as the V, but it occurs infrequently as the cadential chord in a half cadence.

III. Since the V7 is a four-tone chord, all four tones may be present. In many situations the root is doubled and the fifth omitted (see IV–B).

IV. The basic voice-leading rules for connecting I–V apply with the following observations.

    A.   The seventh of the chord may be introduced melodically by step from above or below, or by leap.

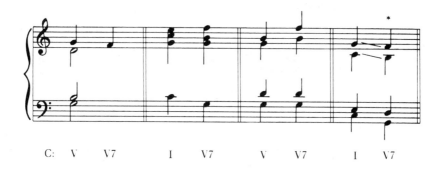

C: V   V7   I   V7   V   V7   I   V7

    B.   The voice leading in the progression V7–I is determined by the need to resolve the dissonant intervals. The third and seventh of the V7 are tendency tones. When both tendency tones in the V7 resolve properly, the tritone formed by these tones is resolved. Note that the d5 contracts to a third, and the A4 expands to a sixth. The normal resolution of the seventh is stepwise downward. The third of the chord (the leading tone) resolves to the tonic. The root of the V7 in the bass moves to the root of I. In an incomplete V7, the doubled root remains stationary. This is referred to as the *strict resolution* of the dominant seventh chord.

---

*A perfect fifth may move to a diminished fifth if the diminished fifth is subsequently resolved.

C: V7   I

At this point, do exercise 1 at the end of this unit.

C. Note that if the tritone of a complete V7 is resolved, the fifth will be omitted and the root tripled in the I. However, when the leading tone is in an *inner voice*, it may skip down a third to the fifth of the I, making both chords complete. As indicated earlier, this is referred to as the *free resolution of the leading tone*.

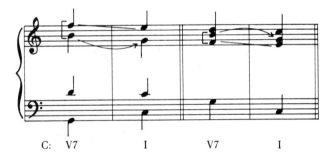

C: V7   I   V7   I

D. In keyboard voicing only, when the chord seventh is in an inner voice, it frequently moves up a step to the fifth of the I. This is referred to as the *free resolution of the seventh*.

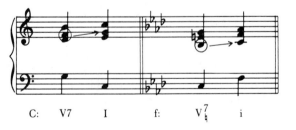

C: V7   I   f: V$^7_\natural$ i

---

*In keyboard voicing, both notes of an implied unison doubling are not commonly written. This results in a momentary reduction to three voices.

E. In the case of chord repetition, the seventh may move from voice to voice. The resolution generally takes place in the last voice in which the seventh appears.

V. The dominant ninth chord (V9).*

A. The V9 consists of a major triad with a minor seventh and a major ninth (MmM9) or a minor seventh and a minor ninth (Mmm9).

B. The V9 is a five-tone chord (when complete) with dominant function. The interval of the ninth is also dissonant and will either be resolved into a dominant seventh prior to resolution to tonic or be resolved directly to the fifth of the I chord. In the former case, the ninth may be understood as a nonharmonic tone.

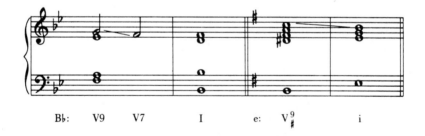

Analysis

Analyze music assigned by the instructor. Refer to the Checklist for Analysis (Part V, Unit 21).

---

*The V9 is included here for completeness and because the chord may occur in the musical examples for analysis. For further discussion, refer to Part III, Unit 7.

Exercises

1. Resolve the following V7 chords in the given voicing. Indicate the tritone with brackets and resolve strictly, as in IV–B.

2. Resolve the following V7 chords in the given voicing. Indicate the tritone with brackets. Resolve the leading tone or chord seventh freely, whichever is appropriate, as in IV–C and IV–D.

3. Resolve the following V7 chords both strictly and freely, as indicated:

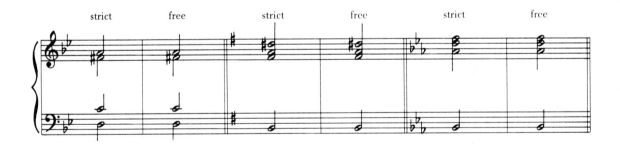

4. Complete the following I–V7 progressions, making the V7 either complete or incomplete, as indicated:

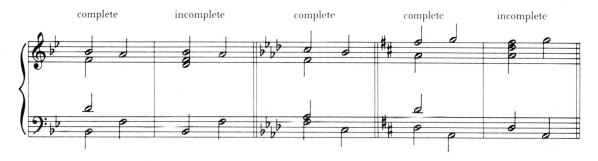

5. Harmonize the following soprano examples in both keyboard and choral voicings, using V7 and I in root position:

6. Harmonize the following melodies, using I, V, and V7 chords in root position. Use the voicing specified by the instructor. Analyze completely, including cadences.

7.   Complete the accompaniment to the given melody. Note that the melody contains passing tones.

8.   Complete the following in the given two-voice texture:

9.   The following patterns may be used for composing melodies, for practice in working with various textures, particularly two-voice textures, or for improvisation. Be conscious of motivic consistency, direction of line, rhythmic continuity, and clarity of cadence. Refer to Part V, Unit 12, for a discussion of expansion and elaboration models.

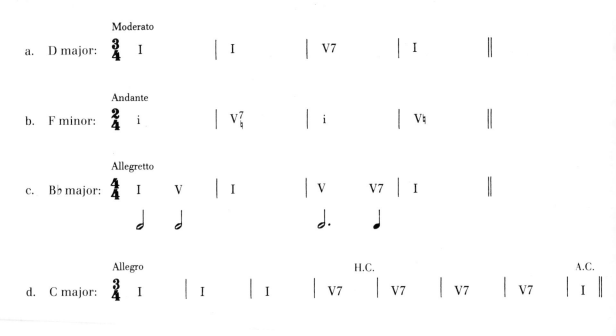

5 Connection of Tonic and Subdominant Triads in Root Position

C: IV   c: iv

I. The roman numerals IV and iv refer to the major and minor triads, respectively, built on the fourth degree of the scale *(subdominant triads)*.

II. The IV chord may be preceded or followed by the I chord. When the I chord is preceded by the IV chord at the end of a phrase, it is termed a *plagal cadence* (P.C.).

III. The same basic procedures employed in I–V connections are to be employed here.

    A. The common tone connection procedure is the same for I–V and I–IV connections.

G: I   IV   d: iv   i   a: i   iv

    B. The noncommon tone connection procedure is the same for I–V and I–IV connections.

Bb: I   IV   g: iv   i   E: IV   I

Exercises

Harmonize the following soprano examples, employing only the tonic and subdominant triads. Use a variety of voicings and spacings.

F: bb: i   iv   E: C: d:

b: f#:   Eb: IV I IV G: g#:

6 Connection of Subdominant and Dominant Triads in Root Position

I. The IV chord frequently functions as a dominant preparation, progressing to V. It rarely follows V.

II. The three upper voices move contrary to the bass to the nearest notes of the second chord. (*Note*: In the much rarer progression V–IV, the procedure is the same.)

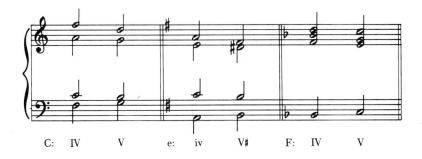

C: IV   V   e: iv   V♯   F: IV   V

The following are common connections of IV to V7:

c: iv   V$^7_♮$ A: IV   V7   B♭: IV   V7

d: iv   V$^7_♯$ E♭: IV   V7   G: IV   V7

Analysis

Analyze music assigned by the instructor. In this and all subsequent music discussed in class, consider the following:

1. What is the rate of chord change (harmonic rhythm)?

2. Is it consistent, or does it change at some point in the phrase?

Exercises

1. Harmonize the following soprano examples, employing only the subdominant and dominant triads and the dominant seventh chord. Use a variety of voicings and spacings.

2. Harmonize the following melodies. Wherever an asterisk occurs, a IV chord is required. Use voicing as specified by the instructor.

a.

b.

c.

I   IV   V7

d.

3. Complete the following in the given texture:

4. The following patterns may be used for composing melodies, for practice in working with various textures, or for improvisation:

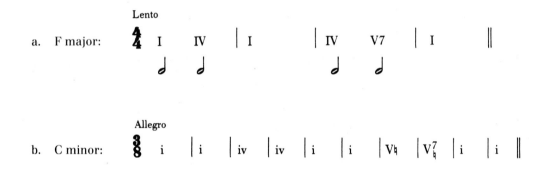

7 Cadences Employing the Tonic, Subdominant, and Dominant Triads in Root Position

Progressions that are used to articulate the ends of phrases (points of arrival or rest in the musical flow) are termed *cadences*. For a complete discussion of cadences, see Part V, Unit 13.

I. A *perfect authentic cadence* (P.A.C.) employs the progression V(or V7)–I, with the first scale-degree in the soprano in the I chord. Both chords must be in root position.

G: V7   I   e: V♯   i

II. An *imperfect authentic cadence* (I.A.C.) employs the progression V(orV7)–I, with the third or fifth scale-degree in the soprano in the I chord.

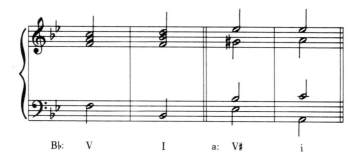

B♭: V   I   a: V♯   i

III. A *half cadence* (H.C.) employs a progression ending on V.

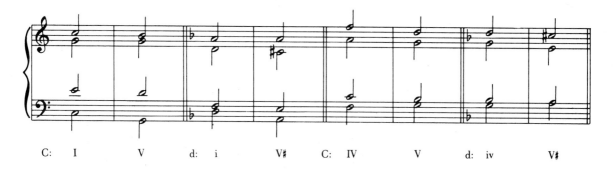

C: I   V   d: i   V♯   C: IV   V   d: iv   V♯

53

IV. A *plagal cadence* (P.C.) employs the progression IV–I.

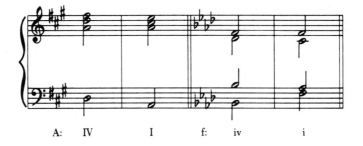

A: IV   I   f: iv   i

Analysis

Analyze music assigned by the instructor. In addition to the items included to this point, consider the following:

1. What types of cadences are used, and where do they occur?

2. How long are the phrases?

3. Are the phrases related?

4. Do the phrases form a period? Of what type?

Exercises

1. Construct the following cadence formulas:

    P.A.C. in E minor   P.A.C. in A♭ major
    H.C. in B♭ major   P.C. in D minor
    P.C. in A minor   I.A.C. in G major
    I.A.C. in F♯ minor   H.C. in C♯ minor
    H.C. in B♭ minor   P.A.C. in E major

2. Compose four-measure phrases ending with the following cadence formulas. Employ textures specified by the instructor. Be attentive to harmonic rhythm, motivic consistency, and rhythmic continuity.

    P.A.C. in D major
    H.C. in G minor
    I.A.C. in E♭ major
    P.C. in B major

3. Compose an eight-measure period for piano, the first phrase ending with an H.C. and the second, with a P.A.C. Edit fully and specifically, including tempo, phrasing, and dynamics. (*Note*: The following units in Part V will be helpful: Unit 11, Unit 13, and Unit 17.)

8 The Cadential Tonic Six-Four Chord

I. The *tonic six-four chord* (I$_4^6$) is a triad in *second inversion*, a triad arranged so that its fifth is in the bass; note the intervals of the sixth and fourth above the lowest note. The fourth in this context is a dissonant interval.

II. In common usage most six-four chords are considered nonfunctional (*linear*), since the tones in the upper voices can be analyzed as nonharmonic (passing tone, neighboring tone, and so forth). The *cadential tonic six-four chord* usually immediately precedes the V or V7 at an authentic or half cadence, and the sixth and fourth above the bass function as melodic embellishments to tones of the dominant (either as appoggiaturas or suspensions). All linear chords are analyzed in brackets, and their type of use is indicated. Other linear six-four chords are discussed in Part II, Unit 12.

III. Normally, the fifth of the chord (that tone in the bass) is doubled.

C: $\left[I_4^6 \right]$

IV. Voice leading.

    A. The following occur in normal resolution.
       1. The bass remains stationary.
       2. The intervals of the sixth and fourth above the bass move stepwise downwards.
       3. The doubled fifth may remain stationary or move to the seventh of the V7.
       4. The chord is metrically stronger than the chord of resolution.

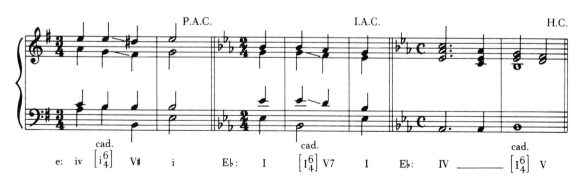

B. When resolution is to V7, the sixth above the bass may move up stepwise to the chord seventh. This generally occurs when the sixth is in an inner voice.

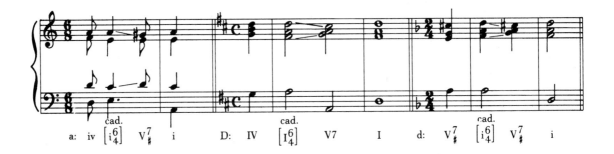

Analysis

Analyze music assigned by the instructor, referring to the Checklist for Analysis (Part V, Unit 21). Bring further examples from the literature into class.

Exercises

1. Harmonize the following sopranos in a variety of voicings and spacings and using tonic six-four chords where indicated by an asterisk.

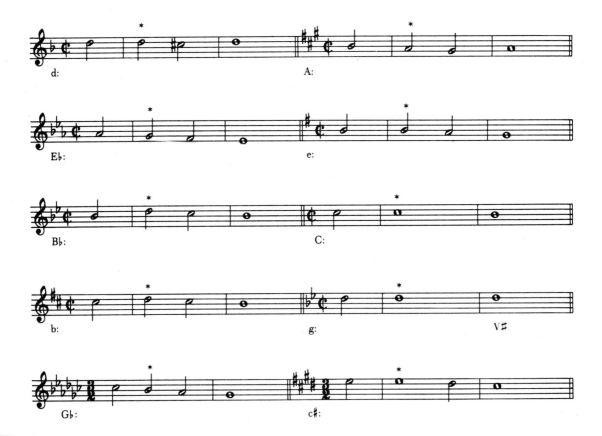

2.   Harmonize the following melodies, employing tonic six-four chords where indicated by the asterisks. Analyze fully.

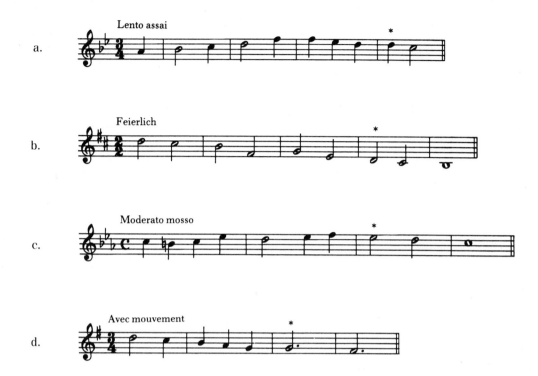

3.   Continue the harmonization of the given melody in the texture and style indicated by the opening bars. Use the complete harmonic vocabulary studied to date, and include at least one cadential six-four chord. Score your results for instruments available in class. Information on ranges and transpositions can be found in Part V, Unit 23; explanation and examples for analysis of chordal textures can be found in Part V, Unit 17.

Alla Britannia

4. Compose an original chorale for either instruments or chorus consisting of an eight-bar period, the first phrase ending on a half cadence and the second phrase ending on a perfect authentic cadence. Edit fully. Units 13 and 23 of Part V will be helpful.

5. The following patterns may be used for composition or improvisation.

   a. D major:

   b. G minor:

   c. Db major:

9 Tonic, Subdominant, and Dominant Triads in First Inversion

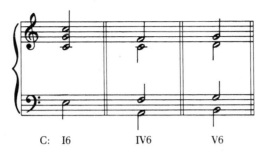

C: I6   IV6   V6

I. A chord in *first inversion* (sixth chord) is one arranged so that its third is in the bass. The *6* beside the roman numeral in the analysis indicates that the root is a sixth above the bass. Refer to Part V, Unit 9, for further discussion of figured-bass symbols.

II. A chord in first inversion has the same function as that chord in root position. The final chord of a cadence is rarely in inversion. A V6–I progression at a cadence point forms an imperfect authentic cadence. (See Part V, Unit 13.)

III. Doubling.

    A. Root doubling is preferable.

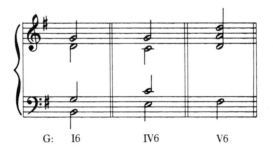

G: I6   IV6   V6

In keyboard voicings, unison doublings are often implicit, rather than written out.

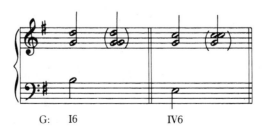

G: I6   IV6

B. Fifth doubling is next in preference.

f: i6   iv6   V6

C. Third doubling is the least preferable (in the V chord, the leading tone is not to be doubled).

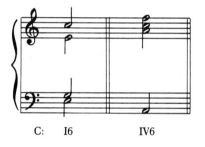

C: I6   IV6

IV. As with progressions of triads in root position, smoothness of line is a major consideration in first inversion. Thus progression to the nearest appropriate spacing and doubling of the succeeding chord is the normal procedure in voice leading.

V. The need for a more melodic bass line results in the use of chords in first inversion. Some characteristic bass-line patterns are illustrated below. Circled numbers indicate scale degrees in the bass.

A. I6

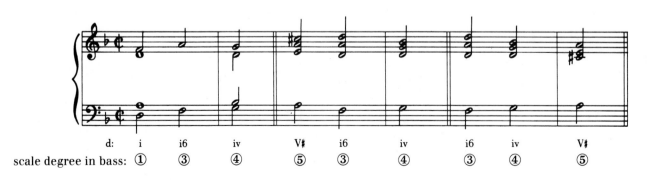

d: i   i6   iv   V♯   i6   iv   i6   iv   V♯

scale degree in bass: ①   ③   ④   ⑤   ③   ④   ③   ④   ⑤

B. IV6

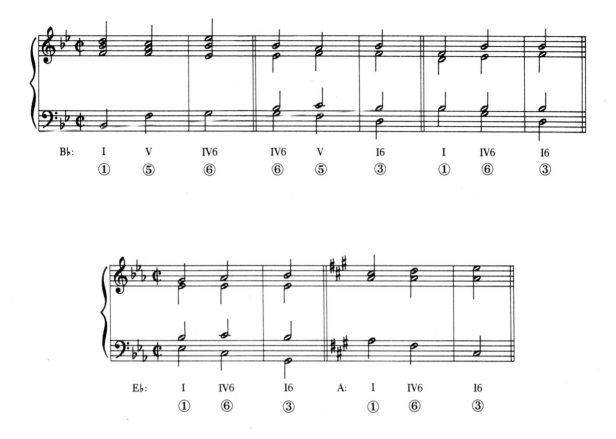

1. A IV6 chord used to resolve a V or V7 chord is called a *deceptive resolution*. When this progression occurs at the end of a phrase, the resulting cadence is called a *deceptive cadence (D.C.)*. Other possibilities for deceptive resolutions will be found in later units.

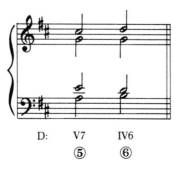

2. The progression iv6–V in a minor key, when used as a terminal progression, is sometimes called a *phrygian cadence*. It is typically used in Baroque compositions to close a middle movement of a larger work.

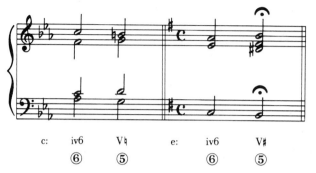

C. V6. In the following examples, note that successive first inversion chords require a change of doubling or spacing to avoid parallel fifths and/or octaves.

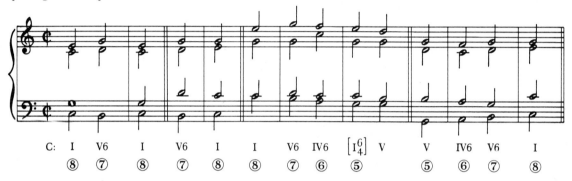

D. Temporary reduction to three-voice texture for consecutive sixth chords is typical of keyboard writing.

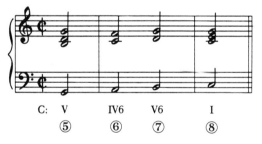

VI. The following example incorporates the most common first-inversion idioms. Note the bass scale degrees associated with these idioms.

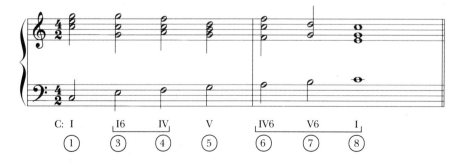

VII. At this point it is advisable to study the guidelines for voice leading and doubling in Part V, Units 5 and 6.

VIII. From now on the fifth, and more rarely the third, may be doubled in I, IV, and V chords in root position to facilitate smoothness of line. The leading tone, however, should not be doubled. See example V–C, above.

IX. Nonharmonic tones (see Part V, Unit 3, for descriptions).

    A. Escape tone (e.t.).

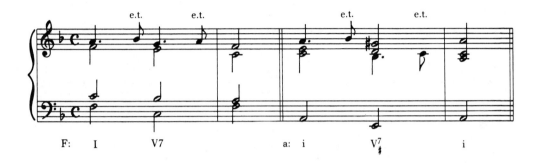

    B. Free neighbor (f.n.)

    C. Anticipation (ant.).

Analysis

Analyze music assigned by the instructor. In this and all subsequent music discussed in class, consider the following, and refer to Part V, Unit 19, for a discussion of counterpoint.

1. What is the contrapuntal relationship between the outer voices?

2. Is the bass primarily functional or linear?

3. Does imitation occur within the texture?

Exercises

1. Realize the following figured basses, employing triads in first inversion as indicated:

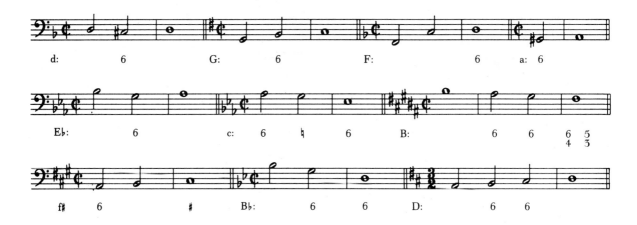

2. In the following progressions, introduce escape tones where indicated by an asterisk:

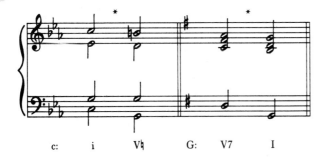

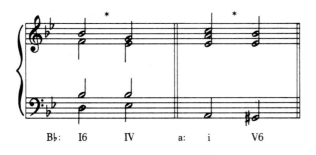

3. In the following progressions, introduce free neighbors where indicated by an asterisk:

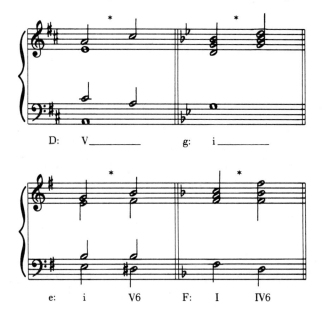

4. In the following progressions, introduce anticipations where indicated by an asterisk:

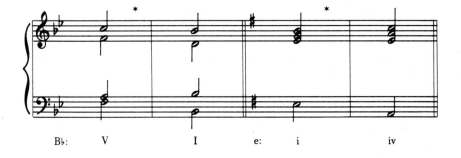

5. Harmonize the following melodies, employing triads in first inversion where appropriate. Employ non-harmonic tones. Strive for a musical bass line, being attentive to the counterpoint between the outer voices. Analyze all work completely.

    a.

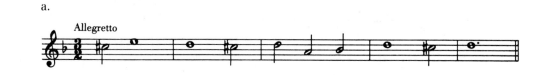

b.

c.

d.

6. Realize the following figured basses. Employ nonharmonic tones. Work for a musical soprano melody, being attentive to the counterpoint between the outer voices. Analyze all work completely. For an explanation of figured-bass symbols, refer to Part V, Unit 9; refer to Part V, Unit 10, for the procedure in harmonizing a figured bass. Some of these basses may be worked out in two- or three-voice contrapuntal texture, as indicated by the instructor; no imitation is required. See Part V, Unit 19, for a discussion of counterpoint.

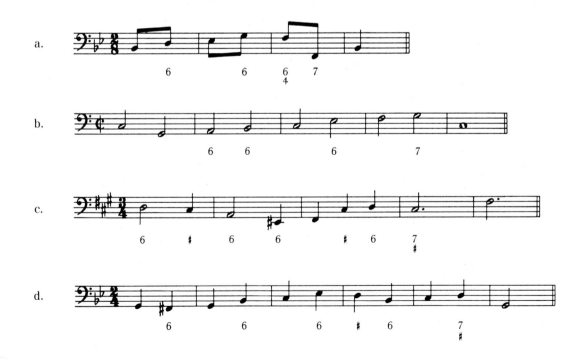

7. Study examples of ground bass (basso ostinato) from the literature, and compose a passacaglia using the following ground bass. Refer to Part V, Unit 19, for a discussion of counterpoint.

8. Complete the following two-voice contrapuntal exercises.

    a.

    b.

    (unfigured)

9. Harmonize the following unfigured basses. Employ triads in first inversion where appropriate, supplying figures and analyzing completely. Work for a musical soprano melody, being attentive to the counterpoint between the outer voices.

    a.

    b.

10 The Supertonic Triad

C: ii   ii6   c: ii°   ii°6

I. The *supertonic triad* is a minor triad in the major mode and a diminished triad (indicated by the symbol °) in the minor mode. In the minor mode the supertonic triad is most frequently found in first inversion so that the dissonant tritone is not formed with the bass.

II. The supertonic triad will generally function as a dominant preparation, a progression analogous to IV–V.

III. Doubling.

   A. ii in root position: Doubled root is preferable, and third or fifth is next.

   B. ii in first inversion: Doubled third is preferable, and root or fifth is next.

   C. ii° and ii°6: Doubled third is preferable; the root is doubled occasionally, but never the fifth.

IV. The supertonic triad may be preceded by tonic or subdominant chords.

   A. When moving from tonic to supertonic, both in root position, upper voices generally move contrary to the bass, but the third of the I may move to the third of the ii.

C: I   ii   a: i   ii°

   B. When moving from subdominant to supertonic, both in root position, hold the common tones.

C: IV   ii   A: IV   ii

C. When either chord is in inversion, move in the smoothest way.

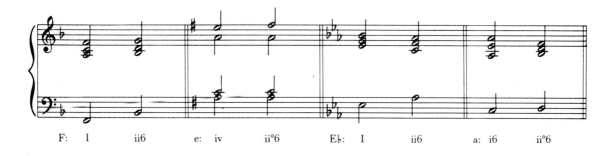

F: I   ii6   e: iv   ii°6   E♭:   I   ii6   a: i6   ii°6

V. Connection of the supertonic triad with V and V7.

A. Supertonic triad in root position.
   1. The bass moves from the root of ii to the root of V.
   2. Upper voices move in contrary motion to the nearest chord tone.
   3. The third of ii may remain stationary, becoming the seventh of V7.
   4. The fifth of ii° in the minor mode is a tendency tone, usually resolving downward to the root of V.

C: ii   V   e: ii°   V♯   B♭: ii   V   A: ii   V7   B♭ ii   cad.⌈I⁶₄⌉ V

   5. The common tone connection can be used only when the quality of the ii is minor. A doubled root allows one tone to leap to the seventh of the V7 or remain stationary.

E♭: ii   V   E♭: ii   V7   D: ii   V7   I   D: ii   V   I

B. Supertonic triad in first inversion.

   1. Voice leading is analogous to the IV–V progression. Note the doubling; here again, a doubled root may leap or remain stationary.

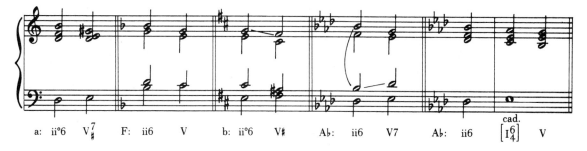

   2. Common tone connection in major mode.

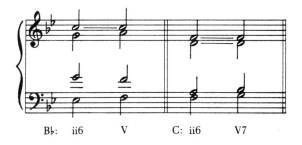

   3. In the common tone connection in minor mode, note that the fifth of the supertonic triad must resolve down to avoid the augmented second.

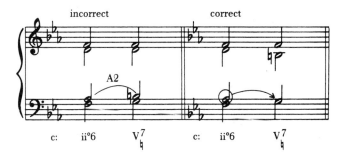

Analysis

Analyze music assigned by the instructor. Refer to the Checklist for Analysis (Part V, Unit 21). Bring other examples from the literature into class.

Exercises

1. Harmonize the following sopranos in both keyboard and choral voicing.

   a. Use ii in root position where indicated by the asterisk.

g: a:

b.   Use ii in first inversion where indicated by the asterisk.

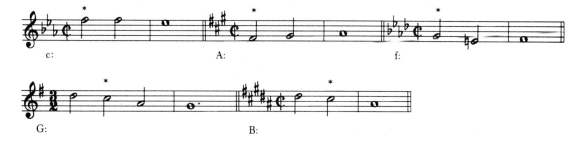

c: A: f:

G: B:

2.   Realize the following figured basses, employing nonharmonic tones where appropriate. Strive for a musical melody line, and analyze all work completely. Some of these may be worked out in two- or three-voice contrapuntal texture.

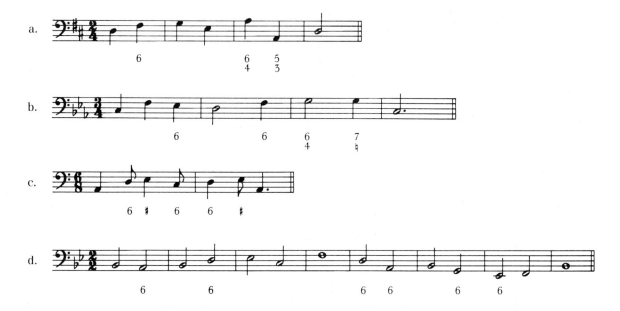

3.   Harmonize the following melodies. Work for a musical bass line, and analyze all work completely. Refer to Part V, Units 8 and 11, for discussions of chord functions and harmonizing a melody.

4. Complete the following in the given texture:

5. Complete the following contrapuntal exercises:

a.

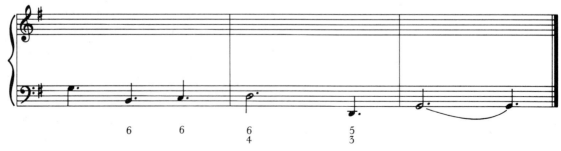

b.

(unfigured)

6. The following patterns may be used for composition or improvisation.

a. B major:

Maestoso

¢ I | I | ii6 | V | ii | ii | V | I ‖

b. E minor:

Allegretto

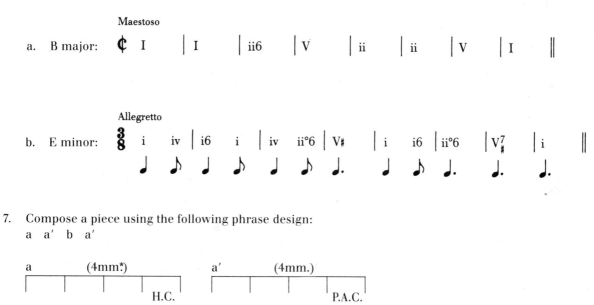

7. Compose a piece using the following phrase design:
   a a′ b a′

a   (4mm.*)   a′   (4mm.)

            H.C.   P.A.C.

b   (4mm.)   a′   (4mm.)

            H.C.   P.A.C.

_____

*mm. = measures.

11 Inversions of the Dominant Seventh Chord

I. In the inversions of the dominant seventh chord, the tritone is resolved in the same manner as the root position dominant seventh chord.

A. In the first inversion, V^6_5, the third is in the bass; figures represent the intervals of the root (6) and seventh (5) above the bass.

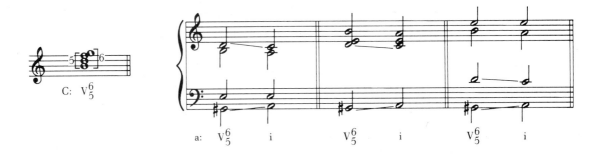

B. In the second inversion, $V^{(6)}_4{}_3$, the fifth is in the bass; figures represent the intervals of the root (4) and seventh (3) above the bass. The figure 6 is normally used only in the minor mode to indicate alteration of the leading tone. A slash through a figure means that the note is to be raised a half step.

---

*Note the doubled third, which often occurs in the resolution of the V^4_3.

Note the exceptional resolution of the seventh in the progression I–V$^4_3$–I6, resulting from parallel tenths in the bass and soprano.

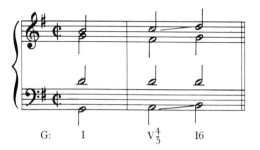

G: I   V$^4_3$ I6

C. In the third inversion, V($^4_2$), the seventh is in the bass; the figure represents the interval of the root above the bass (2). The figure 4 is normally used only in the minor mode to indicate the alteration of the leading tone.

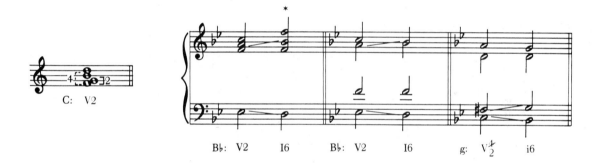

C: V2

Bb: V2   I6   Bb: V2   I6   g: V$^{\star}_2$ i6

D. The fifth may be omitted and the root doubled in the V$^6_5$ and the V2.

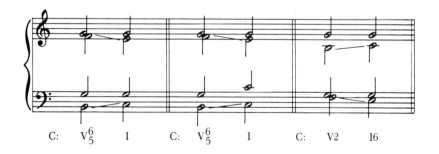

C: V$^6_5$ I   C: V$^6_5$ I   C: V2   I6

_____

*Note the doubled fifth.

E. The following example includes several very common inverted dominant seventh chord idioms, shown bracketed. Note the bass scale degrees associated with these idioms.

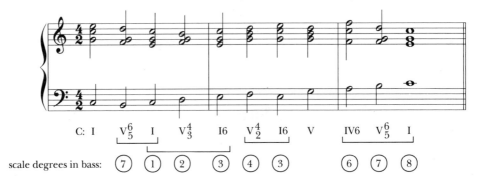

II. Nonharmonic tones (see Part V, Unit 3, for descriptions).

In both the appoggiatura (app.) and the suspension (sus.), the note of resolution should not be doubled unless it is normally doubled in the chord of resolution. It is helpful to observe that the appoggiatura and suspension are similar except that the suspension is prepared.

A. Appoggiatura.

B. Suspension.

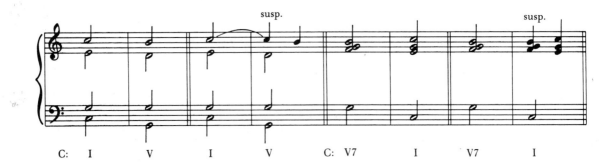

Analysis

Analyze music assigned by the instructor, keeping in mind all the elements previously considered.

Exercises

1. Harmonize the following, employing inversions of the dominant seventh as indicated.

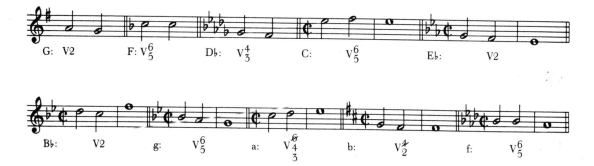

2. In the following progressions, introduce appoggiaturas where indicated by an asterisk:

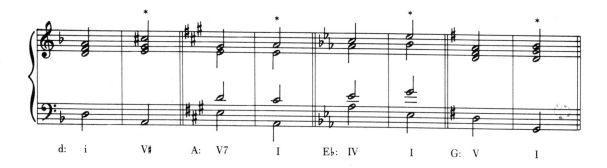

3. In the following progressions, introduce suspensions where indicated by an asterisk:

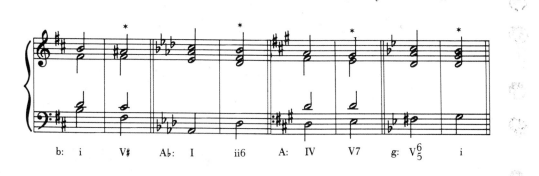

4. Realize the following figured basses. Employ nonharmonic tones. Work for a musical soprano melody, being attentive to the counterpoint between the outer voices. Analyze all work completely. Refer to Part V, Unit 10, for a discussion of harmonizing a figured bass.

a.

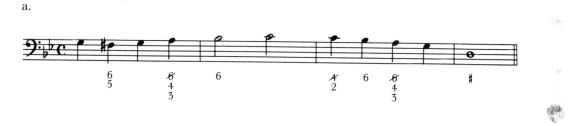

b.

c.

d.

e.

f.

5. Harmonize the following melodies, employing inversions of the dominant seventh chord in places marked with an asterisk. Employ nonharmonic tones. Work for a musical bass line, being attentive to the counterpoint between the outer voices. Refer to Part V, Units 8 and 11, for a discussion of chord functions and harmonizing a melody.

a.

b.

Allegretto

c.

Moderato

d.

Nicht zu schnell

e.

Andante

6. Complete the following to a total length of at least eight measures. Continuing with the given texture, score the example for instruments that are available in class. Refer to Part V, Unit 23, for information on instrumental ranges and transpositions.

Andante

7. Realize the following figured basses in the given contrapuntal textures:

a.

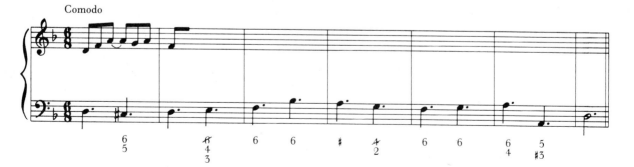

Comodo

b.

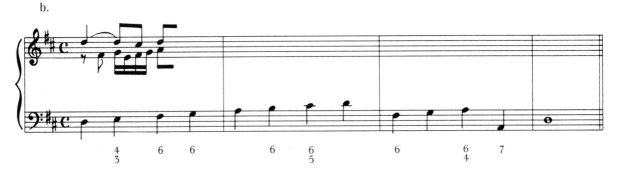

8. Study examples of ground bass (basso ostinato) from the literature. Then compose a passacaglia for organ using the following unfigured bass. Refer to Part V, Unit 19, on counterpoint.

9. In the style of Exercise 6, compose a contrasting period of eight to sixteen measures. End the first phrase with a half cadence and the second with a perfect authentic cadence.

10. The following patterns may be used for composition or improvisation:

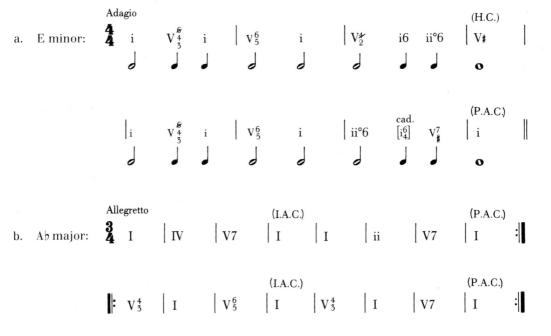

11. Compose a brief binary composition, using the following formal outline.

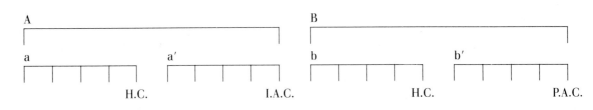

12 Linear (Embellishing) Six-Four and Other Chords

I. Many chord structures may be analyzed as the simultaneous use of several nonharmonic tones. Often the resulting chord structure is recognizable as a particular type of chord (triad, seventh chord, and so forth) but because of its melodic origins is best analyzed as a *linear chord*. This is indicated by placing the roman numeral in brackets along with the designation of the type of nonharmonic use (for example, *n.c.* for *neighboring chord* and *p.c.* for *passing chord*). Included in this category are the various embellishing six-four chords.

A. Neighboring (auxiliary or pedal) chords.
   1. The bass remains stationary.
   2. The upper voices move to neighbors and back. Occasionally one or more upper voices may have passing tones, as in the last example that follows.
   3. The chord generally appears on a weak beat or part of a beat.

B. Passing chords.
   1. The bass moves conjunctly, generally connecting a root position chord with a first inversion chord.
   2. The chord appears on a weak beat or part of a beat.

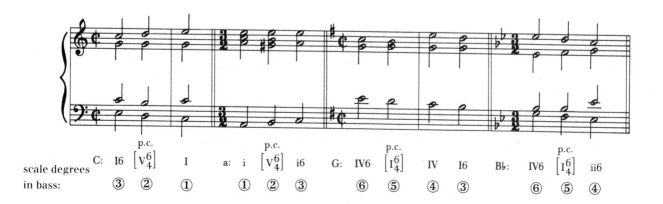

81

C. With appoggiatura or suspension chords, voice leading is analogous to the cadential I$^6_4$, and the chord generally occurs on a strong beat or part of a beat.

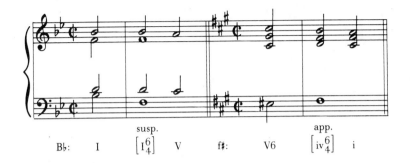

D. Six-four chords may occur as a result of an arpeggiated bass line, with a bass line that alternates between root and fifth in many accompanimental patterns, or when the melody is in the bass.

II. Any chord may be functional or linear, depending on the context. Chords that lack a functional root relationship with the preceding and following chords are often best analyzed as linear. This situation frequently arises with a highly conjunct bass line.

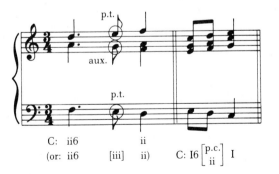

Analysis

Analyze music assigned by the instructor. Refer to the Checklist for Analysis (Part V, Unit 21).

Exercises

1. Realize the following figured basses, paying particular attention to the shape and direction of the melodic line. Analyze completely.

    a.

    b.

2. Harmonize the following melodies, using six-four chords where indicated by an asterisk. Analyze completely.

    a.

    b.

3. Complete the harmonization of the following melody in the given texture. Use linear chords wherever appropriate.

4. Harmonize the following melodies. Tones with asterisks may be treated as simple melodic embellishments (nonharmonic tones) or "harmonized" with other nonharmonic embellishing tones. The resultant sonorities may be analyzed as linear chords. In these melodies and all subsequent melodies with embellishing tones, use the *slowest harmonic rhythm* appropriate to the tempo and character of the melody.

13 Submediant and Mediant Triads in Root Position and First Inversion

I. The roman numerals VI and vi refer to the major and minor triads built on the sixth degree of the scale (*submediant triads*). The roman numerals III and iii refer to the major and minor triads built on the third degree of the scale (*mediant triads*).

II. Progressions.

    A. The VI chord is usually preceded by III, I, or V and is usually followed by II, V, or IV.

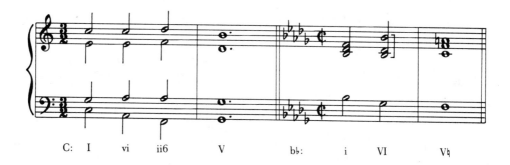

    B. V–VI or V7–VI is a deceptive resolution. When this progression occurs at a cadence point, it is termed a *deceptive cadence (D.C.)*. Note the usual resolution of the leading tone and the seventh of the dominant seventh chord, as well as the resulting doubled third in the submediant.

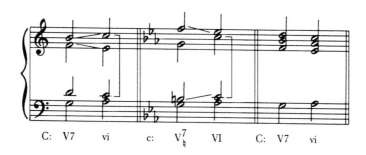

C. The III chord is usually preceded by I or VI and is usually followed by IV or VI.

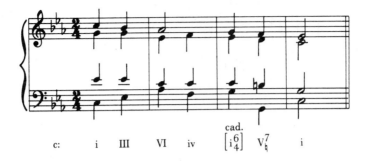

III. Linear uses.

A. The root position VI chord can be used to embellish the I chord.

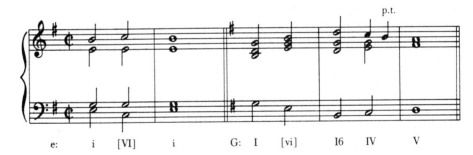

B. Both VI6 and III6 are weak structures; they are rarely independent.

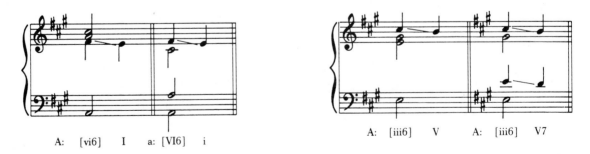

In these instances the mediant and submediant may be understood as linear chords, or the third or sixth scale-degree may be understood as a nonharmonic tone.

Analysis

Analyze music containing phrases of irregular length.

1. Are the phrases shorter or longer than normal?

2. What devices are used to achieve this irregularity?

3. Do the phrases form periodic or phrase-group relationships?

Exercises

1. Realize the following figured basses. (Refer to Part V, Unit 10.) Employ nonharmonic tones, and work for a musical soprano melody. Analyze all work completely.

a.

b.

c.

d.

2. Harmonize the following melodies, employing mediant and submediant triads where appropriate:

a.

b.

Moderato assai

c.

Andantino

d.

Allegretto

e.

Moderato

vi

3. Study examples of nonimitative two-voice counterpoint. Complete the following exercises and analyze fully, being attentive to the rhythmic and intervallic relationships between the voices and to the clarity of the harmonic implications. Refer to Part V, Unit 19, on counterpoint.

a.

b.

4.   Add a bass voice to the given melody. The added voice should be as melodically independent as possible.

5.   Compose a period for an instrumental combination available in class, employing the phrase and cadence structure outlined here. (Refer to Part V, Unit 23, for information on instrumental ranges and transpositions.)

6.   The following patterns may be used for composition or improvisation:

a.   D major:

b. E minor:

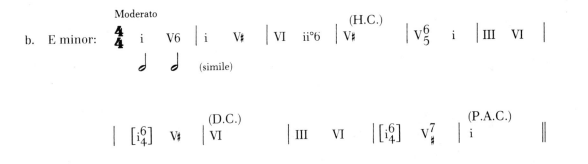

7. Compose a double period for an instrumental combination available in class, employing the period, phrase, and cadence structure outlined here. (Refer to Part V, Unit 25, for information on instrumental ranges and transposition.)

a
H.C.

b
I.A.C.

a
H.C.

c
D.C. P.A.C.

14 The Leading Tone Triad

C: vii°   vii°6   c: vii°   vii°6

I. The *leading tone triad* is a diminished triad; it occurs in both major and minor modes.

II. The chord is used with dominant function except to replace V at a half cadence. It may also be used as a linear (embellishing) chord (still associated with tonic harmony). The triad is found most frequently in first inversion.

III. The third is usually doubled, as the root and fifth are tendency tones.

IV. Voice leading.

    A. The root of the chord (the leading tone) always resolves stepwise upward.

    B. One third of the chord generally moves stepwise downward, whereas the other third moves stepwise upward in contrary motion.

    C. The fifth of the chord, though a tendency tone, typically is freely resolved, moving stepwise up to the fifth of the tonic chord. However, see the third example that follows, in which the tritone in the outer voices resolves.

e: i   [vii°6]   i6   Bb: IV   vii°6   I   F: IV6   vii°   I

cf. V$\frac{4}{3}$

G: I   vii°6   I6

V. A complete summary of part-writing and doubling procedures will be found in Part V, Units 5, 6, and 7.

Analysis

Analyze music assigned by the instructor, keeping in mind all the elements previously considered.

Exercises

1. Realize the following figured and unfigured basses, using nonharmonic tones where appropriate:

   a.

   b.

   c.

   d.

2. Harmonize the following melodies. Three- or four-voice instrumental or keyboard textures may be employed. Analyze all work completely.

   a.

   Andantino

   b.

   Moderato

c.

d.

3. Complete the following fragment in the indicated texture for instruments available in class. Information on ranges and transpositions can be found in Part V, Unit 23; explanation and examples for analysis of three-part texture can be found in Part V, Unit 17.

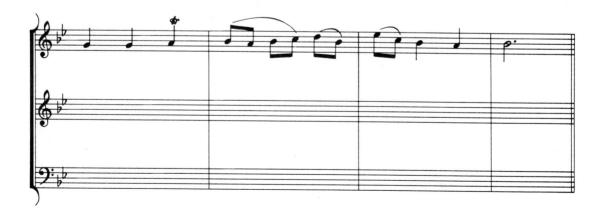

4.   Complete the following in the given contrapuntal textures:

a.

b.

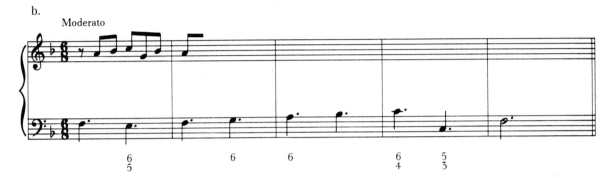

5.   The following patterns may be used for composition or improvisation:

a.   C major: **3/4** I | vii°6 | I6   IV | V   V2 | I6 | IV6   vii°

          | I   IV   V | I   ‖

b.   D minor: ¢   i   i6 | vii°6̸   i | V♯ | V♯ | i | vii°6̸   i6 |

          | iv   V♯ | i   ‖

15 Variant Qualities of Triads

I. Scalar variants

A. The following are variants relating to use of the melodic minor scale. Note that these chords use either the raised form of scale degree 6, or the subtonic.

c: IV♮   ii♮5   vi°   v   VII

IV, ii, and vi° are found with the ascending form of the scale; v is found with the descending form.

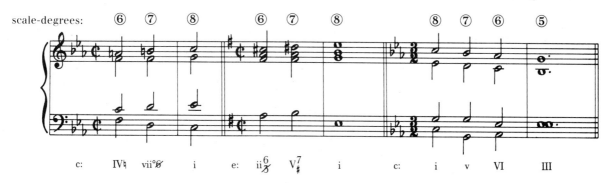

scale-degrees: ⑥ ⑦ ⑧   ⑥ ⑦ ⑧   ⑧ ⑦ ⑥ ⑤

c: IV♮ vii°⑥̷ i   e: ii⑥̷₃ V⁷♯ i   c: i v VI III

d: i   v6   iv6   V♯

⑧ ⑦ ⑥ ⑤

B. The presence of the third scale-degree as a nonharmonic tone over dominant harmony will give the effect of an augmented III + 6. Such sonorities are best understood as V, with the third scale-degree analyzed as nonharmonic.

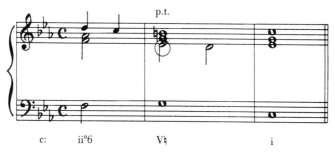

c: ii°6   V♮   i

C. Occasionally a triad will appear over the subtonic in the minor mode (unaltered seventh scale-degree of natural minor). The major triad that results is either associated with a major III chord (with the effect of a momentary shift to the relative major) or with bass motion passing stepwise down from the tonic note. Note that the voice leading in the progression VII–III is analogous to the progression V–I in the relative major and can be analyzed as V/III–III (see Part III, Unit 1).

The progression VII–III often occurs as part of a circle-of-fifths harmonic sequence.

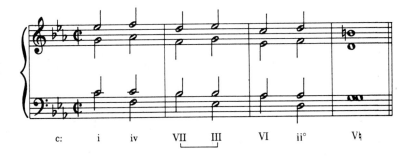

Analysis

Analyze music using scalar variants. Refer to the Checklist for Analysis (Part V, Unit 21).

Exercises

1. Write the following chords in root position using only the treble staff. Add the appropriate accidentals to the roman numerals.

   f: v, ii, VII, IV, vi°.

   c♯: IV, ii, VII, v, IV.

2. Harmonize the following soprano lines, using scalar variants where appropriate.

3. Realize the following figured basses.

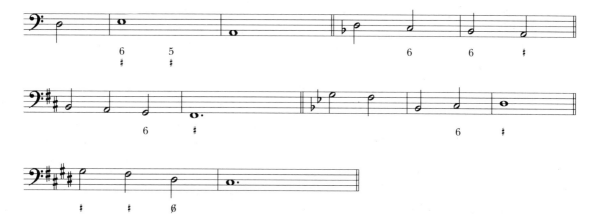

4. Realize the following figured basses.

5. Harmonize the following melodies, using the variant triads discussed in this unit. Analyze completely.

a.

b.

c.

Allegro

d.

Maestoso

II. Modal borrowing (interchange of mode, modal mixture).

A. The modal scale degrees (those which distinguish a major key from its parallel minor) are 3, 6 and 7. For expressive or coloristic reasons, composers sometimes employ modal scale degrees "borrowed" from the parallel key, usually associated with chords borrowed from that key. The function of these chords remains the same. Such borrowed chords are most often found in works in the major mode, and thus come from the parallel minor key. They may be analyzed with the symbol "M.B." and the appropriate roman numeral, with care taken to show the proper chord quality. Note in the following examples the accidentals required in the figured bass.

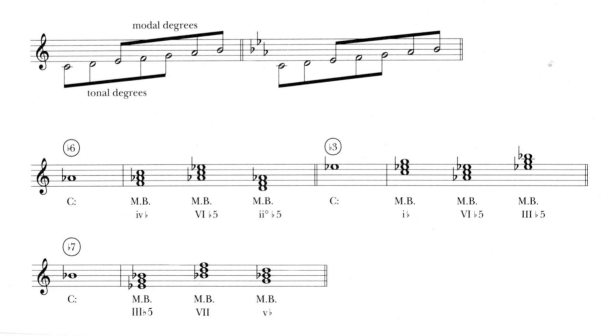

B. Modally borrowed chords may replace or follow the diatonic version of the same chord. They rarely precede the diatonic version.

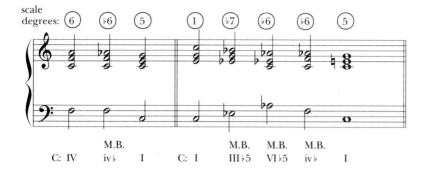

	M.B.				M.B.	M.B.	M.B.	
scale degrees: ⑥	♭⑥	⑤		①	♭⑦	♭⑥	♭⑥	⑤
C: IV	iv♭	I	C: I		III♭5	VI♭5	iv♭	I

C. A work in the minor mode may end on a major tonic triad. The raised third of this chord is called the *Picardy third (tierce de Picardie).* This is the most common borrowing from the parallel major mode.

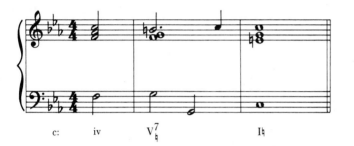

c: iv   V$^{7}_{4}$ I♮

Analysis

Analyze music using modal borrowing. Refer to the Checklist for Analysis (Part V, Unit 21).

Exercises

1. a. Analyze the following modally borrowed chords. Include roman numerals and figured bass with proper accidentals.

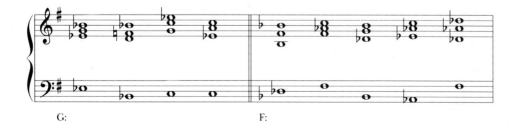

G: F:

b. Alter the following chords by modal borrowing. Analyze both chords of each pair with roman numerals and figured bass symbols, including accidentals.

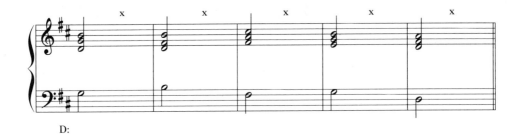

D:

2. Write the following chords in root position, using only the treble staff. Add the appropriate accidentals to the roman numerals.

D: III, iv, i, VI, ii°.
Ab: VII, III, ii°, iv, i.

3. Harmonize the following soprano lines in four voices, using modal borrowing where appropriate. Analyze.

a.

b.

c.

Tempo di minuetto

d.

Andante

4. Realize the following figured basses.

a.

b.

c.

5. Complete the accompaniments to the following melodies in the given textures and styles. Use modally borrowed chords where appropriate.

a.

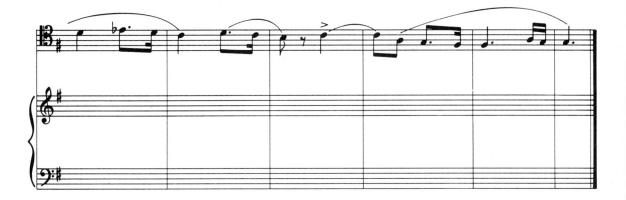

b.

6. The following patterns may be used for composition or improvisation:

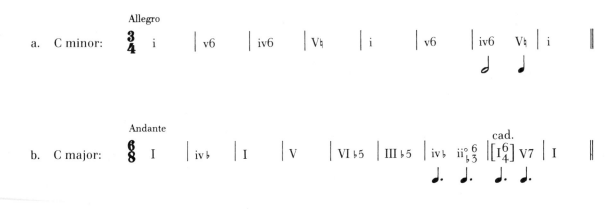

16 The Sequence

I. A *sequence (seq.)* is the repetition of a musical motive or pattern on successively higher or lower pitch levels. Refer to Part V, Unit 16, for further explanation and examples.

II. Sequential progressions.

    A. Sequences may employ functional progressions. When all the diatonic triads occur in this context, the IV and the vii will not have their more usual functions.

    B. The melodic pattern may take precedence over harmonic function, resulting in a linear progression. In this case, the harmonies preceding and following the sequence will be functional.

III. Sequences generally involve a minimum of two and a maximum of four statements of the sequential unit.

Analysis

Look at music containing sequences.

1. What is the sequential unit?

2. How many times is it stated?

3. By what interval is it transposed?

4. What type of progression is employed?

Exercises

1. Continue the given patterns in each sequence. Conclude each pattern with an appropriate cadence, and analyze all work completely.

2. Harmonize the following melodies containing sequences:

a.

b.

Moderato

c.

Lento

VI

d.

Grazioso

3. Realize the following figured and unfigured basses using contrapuntal textures if desired. Employ sequence in the upper voices where the bass is sequential.

a.

b.

4. Complete the following in the indicated texture:

5. Use the following patterns as the basis for sequential elaboration. The progressions may be written out using a variety of textures or improvised using keyboard alone or keyboard with instruments.

a. G minor: $\frac{2}{4}$ i iv | VII III | VI ii° | V♯ VI | iv V♯ | i ‖
♩ ♩ or ♩. ♪

Moderato

b. A♭ major: $\frac{3}{4}$ I | V iii | IV ii | V V7 | I ‖
♩ ♩ ♩ ♩ ♩ ♩

Allegro ma non troppo

c. C major: $\frac{4}{4}$ I V V2 | I6 I | ii6 ii | iii6 iii |
♩ ♩ ♩ ♩ ♩ ♩ ♩ ♩ ♩

[cad.]
| IV6 IV | ii ii6 [I$^6_4$] V7 | I ‖
♩ ♩ ♩ ♩ ♩ ♩

6. Compose original melodies employing sequential patterns, and harmonize accordingly. These examples may be written for piano or for instruments available in class.

17 The Supertonic Seventh Chord

C: ii7   c: ii°7

I. In the major mode the *supertonic seventh chord* is a minor triad with a minor seventh (mm7 or m7), commonly termed a *minor seventh chord*. In the minor mode it is a diminished triad with a minor seventh (dm7), commonly termed a *half diminished seventh chord* (indicated by the symbol °). The ii°7 is often found as a borrowed chord in the major mode.

II. A supertonic seventh chord normally resolves to V or V7.

III. Voice leading.

   A. Supertonic to dominant.
      1. The chord seventh resolves stepwise downward.
      2. The fifth moves stepwise downward or skips to the seventh of the V7.
      3. The third may skip down or remain stationary, becoming the seventh of the V7. In first inversion the third moves stepwise upward to the root of the V.
      4. The root moves to the root of V or remains stationary.

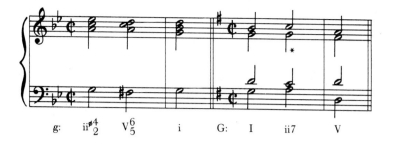

g: ii$^{ø4}_{2}$ V$^{6}_{5}$ i   G: I   ii7   V

B. The linear ii7 chord may occur as a neighboring or a passing chord. The second example that follows is a characteristic three-voice progression occurring most frequently in keyboard textures:

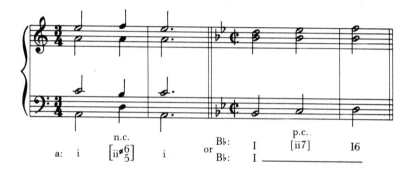

           n.c.   p.c.

a: i   [ii$^{ø6}_{5}$] i   or B♭: I   [ii7]   I6

                               B♭: I

C. A plagal cadence may employ the progression ii$^{6}_{5}$-I:

F: ii $^{6}_{5}$ I   b: ii$^{ø6}_{5}$ i

Analysis

Analyze music assigned by the instructor. Be sure to consider the underlying structural elements as well as the surface detail.

---

*Here the third is doubled (and the fifth omitted) to avoid parallel fifths from I to ii7.

Exercises

1. Harmonize the following sopranos in both keyboard and choral voicing. Use a ii7 wherever indicated by an asterisk. Use a variety of inversions as well as root position; some of the inversions are indicated. Analyze completely.

2. Realize the following figured basses:

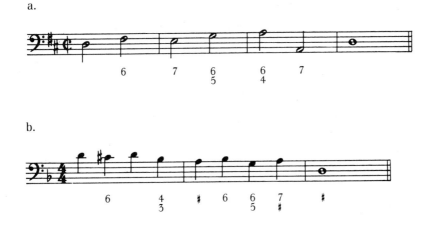

c.

6   7   4 7   6   6   6   6 [7]   6   7   6   7
         3   5   (I————)   5   ♭5   4   3

3. Complete the realization of the following figured bass in the given texture. Then compose an *espressivo*
    solo line for an instrument available in class.

4. Complete the following in the given contrapuntal textures:
    a.

    b.

5. Compose a solo for voice with piano accompaniment using a brief three- or four-line poem in the form a a′ b. Refer to Part V, Unit 20, for a discussion of bar form.

6. The following patterns may be used for composition or improvisation:

Allegro

a. D minor: $\mathbf{C}$ i | i | ii$^{ø4}_{2}$ | ii$^{ø4}_{2}$ | V$^{6}_{5}$ | V$^{7}_{\sharp}$ | ii$^{ø6}_{5}$ V$^{7}_{\sharp}$ | i ‖

Siciliano

b. G major: $\mathbf{^{3}_{8}}$ I | I | ii$^{6}_{5}$ | V | V | vi | ii$^{6}_{5}$ V7 | I ‖

18 The Leading Tone Seventh Chord

I. A seventh chord built on the seventh scale-degree is a *leading tone seventh chord.*

    A. In the minor mode it is a diminished triad with a diminished seventh (dd7), commonly termed a *fully diminished seventh (vii°7).*

        c: vii°7

        1. The root of the vii°7 is always the *raised* form of the seventh scale-degree (the leading tone).
        2. The chord is always fully diminished.

    B. In the major mode it is a diminished triad with a diminished seventh (dd7), or a diminished triad with a minor seventh (dm7), commonly termed a *half diminished seventh (vii⌀7).*

        C: vii°♭7   vii♯7

        1. The chord can be either fully or half diminished.
        2. The fully diminished seventh requires that the sixth scale-degree (seventh of the chord) be lowered chromatically. This may be understood as a modally borrowed chord.

II. The leading tone seventh chord has a dominant function. It may be used in place of a dominant triad or seventh chord, although it is rarely used as the final chord of a half cadence.

III. Normal resolution is to a tonic triad. Because the root, fifth, and seventh are tendency tones, their resolution is usually strictly observed.

    A. For the fully diminished seventh, the seventh resolves down by step, the fifth resolves down by step, the third resolves up or down, and the root resolves up by step.

        c: vii°7   i   vii°7   i   vii°7   i

B. For the half diminished seventh, resolution is the same as for the fully diminished chord except that when the chord third is below the seventh, it cannot resolve down by step because of the parallel perfect fifths that would result. The third must therefore resolve up by step or must be placed above the seventh.

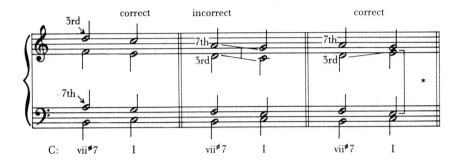

IV. Resolving tendencies are not affected by inversion.

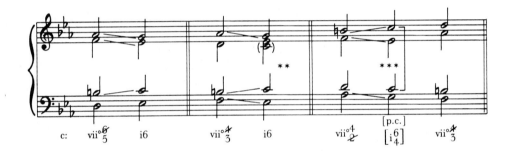

Analysis

Analyze music assigned by the instructor. Refer to the Checklist for Analysis (Part V, Unit 21). Bring further examples from the literature into class.

Exercises

1. Spell vii°7 (fully diminished seventh) in root position and resolve to tonic, using treble clef and signatures, in the following keys: d, D, f, F, e, E, E♭, and e♭.

---

*Note the doubled third.
**Motion from the diminished fifth into the perfect fifth is often accepted when not between the outer voices.
***Note the doubled root.

2. Resolve the leading tone seventh chord as indicated, and analyze.

g: i   i   i6 $\left[i^6_4 \right]$ i6

A♭:   I   I6   I6 $\left[I^6_4 \right]$ I6

3. Harmonize the following melodies, using leading tone seventh chords where indicated by an asterisk:

a.

b.

c.

d.

4. Realize the following figured basses, using various textures and instrumental combinations. Work for a musical soprano line and smooth voice leading.

a.

b.

c.

d.

5. Complete the following, using the given texture. Analyze fully.

6. Complete the following in the given contrapuntal textures:

a.

b.

(unfigured)

7. The following patterns may be used for composition or improvisation:

Adagio

a. B minor: $\mathbf{3 \atop 2}$ i | ii°$^6_5$ | V$^7_\sharp$ | VI | iv | vii°7 | i | i ‖

b. C major: Andante cantabile $\mathbf{\frac{4}{2}}$ I | vi | ii6 | [cad]$[I^6_4]$ V | I | ii7 | vii$^{\sharp}$7 | I ‖

c. E minor: Allegro molto $\mathbf{\frac{4}{4}}$ i | vii°7 | vii°7 | i | VI | ii$^{\sharp}$7 | V$\sharp$ | V$\sharp$ ‖

8. Compose a short work for piano or a group of instruments using a texture and pattern suggested by the instructor and employing leading tone seventh chords where appropriate. Use the following formal outline:

a (8 mm.) H.C.⌐ b (8 mm.) I.A.C.⌐ b′ (8 mm.) P.A.C.⌐

9. Compose a double period for an instrumental combination available in class, employing the period, phrase, and cadence structure outlined here.

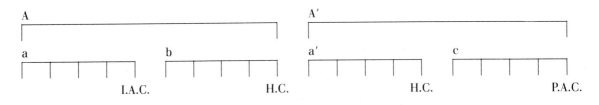

19 Other Diatonic Seventh Chords

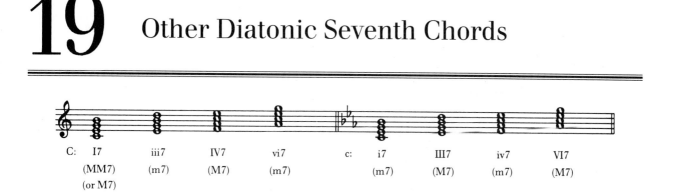

C: I7   iii7   IV7   vi7   c: i7   III7   iv7   VI7
    (MM7) (m7)   (M7)   (m7)   (m7)   (M7)   (m7)   (M7)
    (or M7)

I. A seventh chord may be built on any scale-degree. Of the chords above, the IV7 and vi7 are the most common.

II. The functions of the chords are unaffected by the addition of the seventh.

III. The basic resolution is analogous to the ii7 and V7, with the chord seventh resolving stepwise downward. All diatonic seventh chords occur together most frequently in sequence, going around the circle of fifths. Note that the seventh always resolves regularly and that every other chord is incomplete. All chords will appear complete in thicker textures and in passages in which inversions are used.

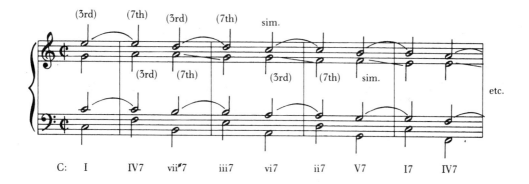

C: I   IV7   vii°7   iii7   vi7   ii7   V7   I7   IV7

IV. A note that appears to be a chord seventh can often be analyzed as a simple nonharmonic tone.

B♭: ii$^6_5$ a: V^7 i

Analysis

Analyze music assigned by the instructor. Refer to the Checklist for Analysis (Part V, Unit 21).

Exercises

1. Realize the following figured basses:

   a.

   b.

   c.

2. Harmonize the following melodies, using seventh chords where indicated by the asterisk. These exercises may be done in a two- or three-voice contrapuntal texture.

   a.

   b.

3. Use the following bass as the basis for sequential elaboration. This exercise may be done in a two-, three-, or four-voice contrapuntal texture.

4. Compose a four-phrase piece with the form a a′ b b′ for instruments available in class. Keep in mind the possibilities of sequence, phrase extension, cadence structure, and so forth. Employ the complete harmonic vocabulary studied to date. Refer to the Composition Checklist (Part V, Unit 22) and Part V, Unit 23, on instrumental ranges and transpositions.

5. The following patterns may be used for composition or improvisation:

    a. F minor:

    Moderato

    $\mathbf{\frac{4}{4}}$ i   iv7 | VII7 III7 | VI7 ii°7 | v7   i7 | iv7   ii°$^6_5$ | $\begin{bmatrix} i^6_4 \end{bmatrix}$ V$^7_{\natural}$ | i   ‖

    b. D major:

    Allegro

    $\mathbf{\frac{3}{4}}$ I | IV$^6_5$ | vii°$^4_2$ | iii$^6_5$ | vi$^4_2$ | ii$^6_5$ | V7 | I   ‖

Part

Chromatic Materials

1 Secondary (Applied, Borrowed) Dominants

I. *Altered chords* are chords having one or more notes that are not in the diatonic scale of the key of a given passage. (The raised forms of the sixth and seventh scale-degrees in minor are considered diatonic.) The most common type of altered chord in tonal music is the *secondary (applied or borrowed) dominant*.

   A. The following are examples of altered chords:

C major

   B. The following are examples of diatonic chords:

C minor

II. Just as the tonic chord is often preceded by its dominant function chords, any major or minor diatonic triad may be preceded by one of its own dominants. For example, the A dominant seventh chord in the following example, found in the key of C major, would be considered altered by virtue of the C♯. It is V7 in the key of D minor. Since the D-minor triad functions as ii in C major, we analyze the altered chord as a *secondary dominant*—V7/ii (read "V7 of ii"). This altered chord could also have other functions in other keys, as follows:

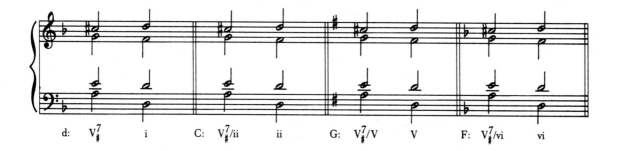

d: $V^7_\sharp$ i   C: $V^7_\sharp$/ii   ii   G: $V^7_\sharp$/V   V   F: $V^7_\sharp$/vi   vi

III. A secondary dominant chord usually resolves to its expected chord of resolution using normal doubling and voice-leading procedures. It may also resolve deceptively, as in the last example that follows:

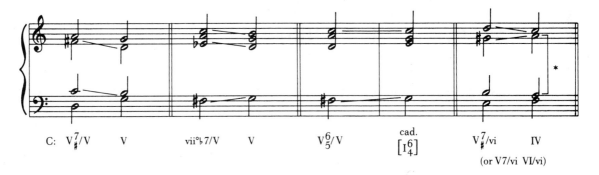

IV. Any chord with dominant *quality* (M, Mm7, d, dd7, dm7, or dominant ninth) may function as a secondary dominant. The half diminished seventh normally resolves to major triads, never to minor triads. The following are the possible chords "of V" in the key of G:

V. A secondary dominant chord may substitute for any diatonic chord with the same function. For instance, vi (which usually resolves to ii or IV) may be replaced by a secondary dominant of ii or IV; ii or IV may be replaced by a secondary dominant of V.

VI. A secondary dominant may progress to another secondary dominant, typically as part of the circle of fifths. For instance, the progression V7/ii–ii may be replaced by V7/ii–V7/V, since the latter chord can be used to replace ii. Furthermore, secondary dominants of any quality may be freely interchanged, as in example B that follows:

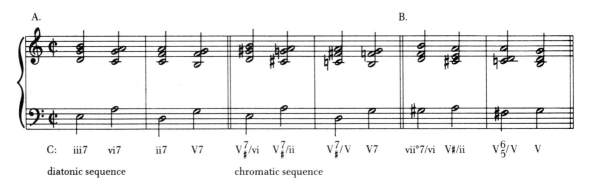

---

*Note doubled third.

VII. Common altered scale-degree formulas follow. These may be useful for determining the harmonic implication of any chromatic note that is clearly a chord tone.

    A. For raised scale-degrees, note that the raised note is usually the third of a V (or V7) sound or the root of a vii°7 (or vii⌀7) sound.

    B. For lowered scale-degrees, note that the lowered note is usually the seventh of either a V7 or vii°7 sound.

VIII. Secondary dominants are sometimes preceded by a dominant preparation, as follows:

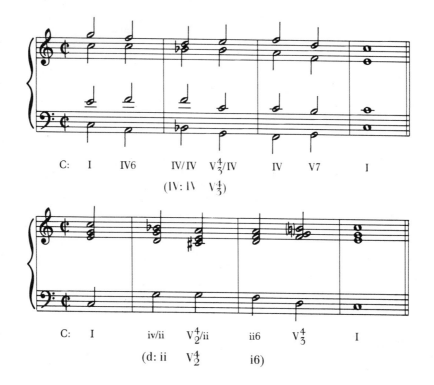

Analysis

Analyze music assigned by the instructor. Consider the following:

1. Where does chromaticism occur?

2. Is the chromaticism essential or embellishing?

3. If it is essential, what harmonic function does it express?

4. Where do the altered chords occur in the phrase?

Exercises

1. Spell the following chords in G major and B♭ major, in root position; use treble clef and key signatures: V7/V, vii°/V, vii°7/V, vii°7/ii, V/vi, V7/iii, and V7/IV.

2. Spell the following chords in E minor and D minor, in root position; use bass clef and key signatures: V/V, V7/iv, V7/VI, vii°7/V, V7/III, and vii°7/III.

3. Explain what functions a dominant seventh chord built on A would have in the following keys: G, g, F, D, C, and B♭. List keys, and analyze functions in roman numerals.

4. Analyze the function of an F♯ fully diminished seventh chord in the following keys: G, g, F, E♭, D, C, c, and B♭.

5. Analyze the given chords and resolve normally.

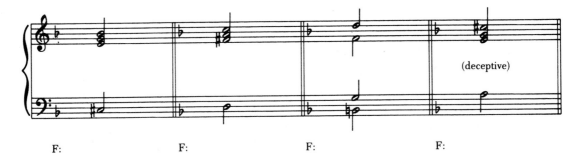

F: F: F: F:

6. Harmonize the following melodies, using secondary dominants in the appropriate places. Analyze fully.

a.

b.

c.

d.

Moderato

e.

Andante

V6   vi

f.

Adagio molto

V$^6_5$/iv

g.

Adagio

mp

7. Work out the following figured and unfigured basses, using textures and instrumentation suggested by the instructor. Strive for a musical melody and a consistent sense of motion. Analyze fully. Refer to Part V, Unit 9, for information on accidentals in figured bass.

a.

b.

c.

d.

e.

f.

g.

8. Add a contrapuntal bass voice to the following melody. Refer to Part V, Unit 19, on counterpoint.

9. Compose a passacaglia on the following bass. Refer to Part V, Unit 19, on counterpoint.

6   4♯2   6   6   ♮   6   6   7♮

10. The following patterns may be used for composition or improvisation:

         Andante

a.   G major: $\mathbf{\frac{3}{4}}$ I | vii°$^7_♮$/ii | ii | V$^6_5$/vi | vi | V$^7_♯$/V | [I$^6_4$]   V7 | I   ‖

         Giga

b.   G minor: $\mathbf{\frac{6}{8}}$ i | V$^7_♮$/iv | iv | V♯ | VI | vii°$^7_♮$/V | [i$^6_4$] | V♯   ‖

         Moderato

c.   A♭ major: $\mathbf{\frac{4}{4}}$ ‖: I | V$^7_♮$/ii | V$^7_♮$/V   V7 | I | I | V$^7_♮$/ii | V$^7_♮$/V | V7 :‖

11. Compose a parallel double period for instruments available in class using secondary dominants where appropriate and based on the following pattern:

        H.C.   I.A.C.   H.C.   P.A.C.

a (4 mm.) ⌐ b (4 mm.) ⌐ a (4 mm.) ⌐ b′ (4 mm.) ⌐

2 Modulation

I. *Modulation* is the process of moving from one tonal center to another, resulting in the clear establishment of the new tonal center. Modulation usually involves three stages: establishment of the first key, the modulatory device, and establishment of the second key.

II. Modulation within the phrase.

   A. Common chord modulation.
   1. The following is a checklist for locating the common (pivot) chord in *common-chord modulation*.
      a. The common chord is *diatonic* in both keys.
      b. The common chord is usually ii or IV in the new key.
      c. . The common chord is usually placed immediately before the first dominant function chord, or I_4^6, in the new key.
      d. The new key is often indicated by a cadential I_4^6 chord.
      e. The new key is usually tonicized by an authentic cadence shortly after the modulation.
      f. All music before the common chord will be functional in the first key; all music from the common chord to the cadence will be functional in the new key.

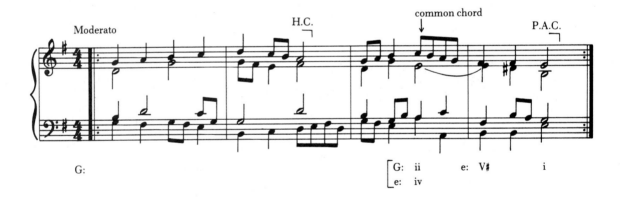

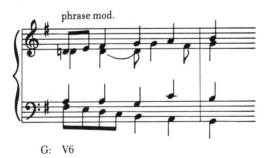

B. Direct modulation. Where direct chromaticism or cross relation occurs at the point of modulation, a *direct (chromatic) modulation* is to be analyzed.

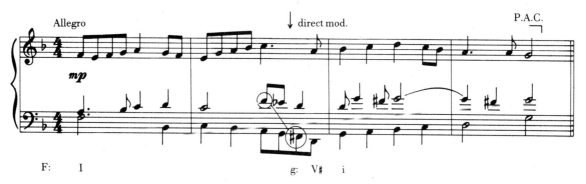

C. Sequential modulation. A sequence passing through a series of secondary dominants may obscure the initial tonality. At any point the sequence may be broken and the new key tonicized by a cadential progression. Refer to the Durante example in Part V, Unit 16.

III. Modulation between phrases. In *phrase modulation*, modulations occur between phrases; that is, a new phrase or section may simply begin in a new key. Even when a potential common chord may be present, such a modulation is analyzed as being of the phrase type. In many small forms, phrase remodulations to the tonic key often occur at the beginning of the second section, as in the example in II–A.

IV. For other means of modulation, see Part III, Unit 6.

V. In analysis, the place where the second key begins is shown in the usual way, with key name and colon, as in II–B. If the modulation is by phrase or is chromatic, a brief note to that effect may be written at that point in the music. If there is a common chord, it is shown with a bracket, as follows:

$$\begin{bmatrix} \text{first key:} \\ \text{second key:} \end{bmatrix} \qquad \text{such as} \qquad \begin{bmatrix} \text{G:} \\ \text{e:} \end{bmatrix}$$

VI. Most modulations are to closely related keys. *Closely related keys* have key signatures that differ by no more than one accidental. The following chart shows the keys considered most closely related to a given main key:

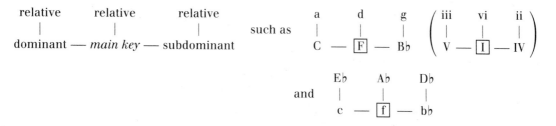

It is possible to modulate to keys other than those that are closely related by means of the devices discussed above.

Analysis

Analyze music assigned by the instructor. Look at several short examples that employ binary and ternary formal processes. Consider the following, and refer to Part V, Units 13, 15, and 20, on cadence and phrase structure, the motive, and form.

1. Where do cadences occur? Of what types and in what keys are they?

2. How many phrases are there? Is there a periodic relationship?

3. How is the first key established?

4. Where do modulations occur? How are they effected?

5. Are the sections motivically or thematically related?

6. Is material restated, varied, or developed?

Exercises

1. Analyze the function of an F-major triad in the following keys: F, f, C, d, E♭, a, D♭, b♭, A♭ and B♭. Which are diatonic?

2. Name the keys in which an F-minor triad could have the following functions: i, ii, iii, iv and vi.

3. Name four diatonic triads that could be used as common chords to modulate between G major and D major, and specify their function in both keys.

4. Apply the preceding question to modulations between the following pairs of keys: g–d, A♭–c, and D–b.

5. Harmonize the following modulating melodies. Work for a musical bass line and good counterpoint between the outer voices. Analyze completely.

a.

b.

c.

d.

e.

f.

g.

h.

i.

6. Work out the following basses, both figured and unfigured, using textures and instrumentation as suggested by the instructor. Work for effective melody lines.

a.

b.

c.

d.

7. Complete the following examples in a two- or three-voice contrapuntal texture:

a.

b.

8. The following patterns may be used for composition and improvisation in a variety of textures, including two- and three-voice counterpoint:

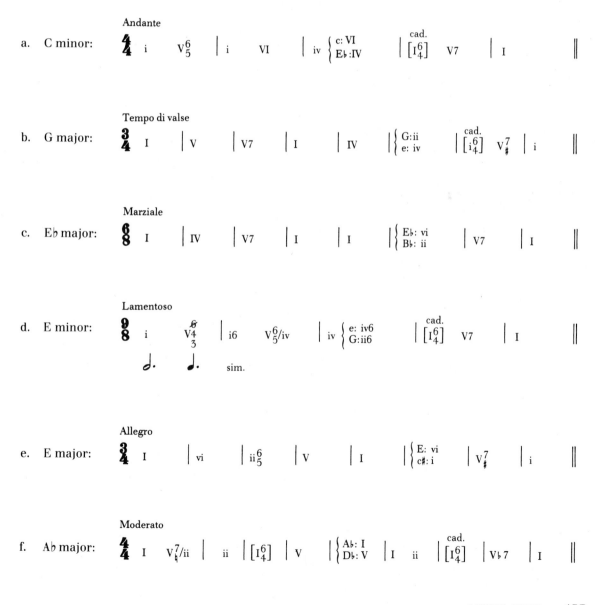

9. Construct original harmonic frameworks of eight to sixteen measures, in roman numerals, modulating between the following pairs of keys: G–e, f–Ab, Bb–c, and D–A. Write melodies based on these frameworks, and harmonize the melodies, using appropriate textures.

10. Analyze simple examples of nonimitative counterpoint as suggested by the instructor. Compose a simple two-voice Baroque binary suite movement, as follows:

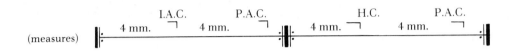

Modulate to the dominant key in the first half and back to the tonic in the second. Refer to Part V, Unit 19, on counterpoint.

3 Linear (Embellishing) Diminished Seventh Chords

I. Simultaneous nonharmonic tones frequently form diminished seventh chords. Like other linear chords, these *linear (embellishing) diminished seventh chords* are analyzed in brackets. Since these chords occur with various enharmonic spellings, they are best analyzed simply by chord quality (dd7) along with the category of nonharmonic tone use.

II. Neighboring (auxiliary) chords.

    A. Embellished major triads.
        1. The root remains stationary.
        2. The third moves to the raised lower neighbor.
        3. The fifth moves to the upper neighbor and/or to the raised lower neighbor.

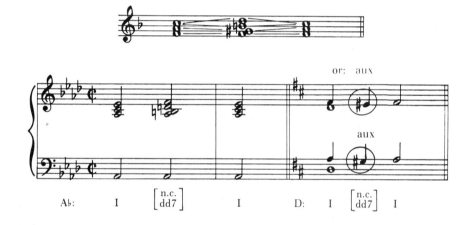

    B. Minor triads rarely have neighboring chords. When they do, both the root and third remain stationary, and the fifth moves up a *major* second and/or down a minor second.

    C. For dominant seventh chords the voice leading is as in the major triad, with the seventh also moving to its lower neighbor.

D. When an inverted triad is embellished, the stationary root will be in one of the upper voices.

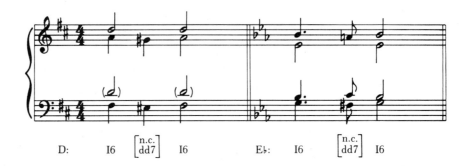

$$
\begin{array}{llll}
\text{D:} & \text{I6} & \begin{bmatrix}\text{n.c.} \\ \text{dd7}\end{bmatrix} & \text{I6} \\
\end{array}
\qquad
\begin{array}{llll}
\text{E}\flat\text{:} & \text{I6} & \begin{bmatrix}\text{n.c.} \\ \text{dd7}\end{bmatrix} & \text{I6} \\
\end{array}
$$

III. Passing chords. When two voices move in parallel 6ths or 10ths, passing chords may result. Note that in the first example, the first of the passing chords is diatonic and the second chromatic.

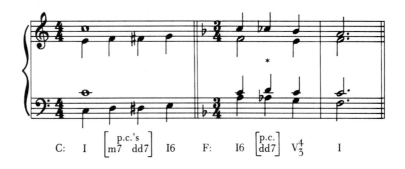

$$
\begin{array}{lllll}
\text{C:} & \text{I} & \begin{bmatrix}\text{p.c.'s} \\ \text{m7} \quad \text{dd7}\end{bmatrix} & \text{I6} \\
\end{array}
\qquad
\begin{array}{lllll}
\text{F:} & \text{I6} & \begin{bmatrix}\text{p.c.} \\ \text{dd7}\end{bmatrix} & \text{V}_3^4 & \text{I} \\
\end{array}
$$

IV. Linear diminished seventh chords may result from combinations of other kinds of nonharmonic tones.

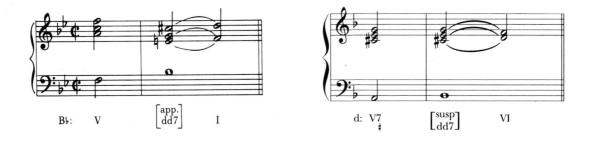

$$
\begin{array}{llll}
\text{B}\flat\text{:} & \text{V} & \begin{bmatrix}\text{app.} \\ \text{dd7}\end{bmatrix} & \text{I} \\
\end{array}
\qquad
\begin{array}{llll}
\text{d:} & \text{V7}_{\sharp} & \begin{bmatrix}\text{susp} \\ \text{dd7}\end{bmatrix} & \text{VI} \\
\end{array}
$$

V. Consecutive stepwise diminished seventh chords may be analyzed either as a series of secondary dominants or as a series of passing chords. Because of spelling discrepancies, however, the latter is generally preferable.

---

*This chord may also be analyzed as a misspelled vii°7/V chord.

D: I   vii°7/ii   vii°7/V   vii°7/vi   vii°7/IV   vii°7/V   vii°$\frac{4}{3}$ I6

or D: I   [passing chords _____]   vii°$\frac{4}{3}$ I6

Analysis

Analyze music assigned by the instructor. In addition to all the matters discussed thus far, consider the following:

1. Where does the chromaticism occur?

2. Is the chromaticism embellishing or essential?

3. If it is embellishing, are linear chords formed?

4. What is the quality of the linear chords?

5. What is their melodic relationship to the chords they embellish?

Exercises

1. Embellish the given chords with neighboring diminished seventh chords where indicated by an asterisk. Analyze completely.

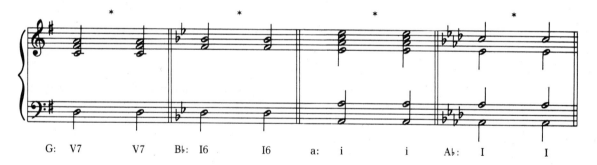

G: V7   V7   Bb: I6   I6   a: i   i   Ab: I   I

2. Add passing chords of any appropriate type where indicated by an asterisk.

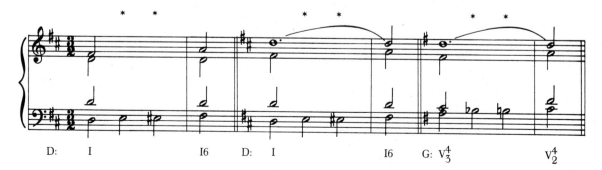

D: I   I6   D: I   I6   G: V$\frac{4}{3}$ V$\frac{4}{2}$

LINEAR (EMBELLISHING) DIMINISHED SEVENTH CHORDS   **141**

3. Where indicated by asterisks, interpolate consecutive stepwise diminished seventh chords between the two chords given. Spelling will be dictated by line. Analyze completely.

Bb: I   V7

4. Embellish the given chords with linear diminished seventh chords where indicated by asterisks.

D: V   I   Eb: V9   I

5. Complete the following for two solo instruments with accompaniment. Use linear diminished seventh chords where appropriate. Edit fully, including phrasing, articulations, and dynamics.

6. Harmonize the following melody in the indicated texture, using linear diminished seventh chords where indicated by an asterisk:

"Les Postludes. . ."

7. Compose an original piece for piano or instruments in a small form. Employ a thick texture containing multiple doublings. Refer to Part V, Units 17, 20, and 22, on texture, form, and composition.

8. The following patterns may be used for composition or improvisation. Add linear diminished seventh chords where appropriate.

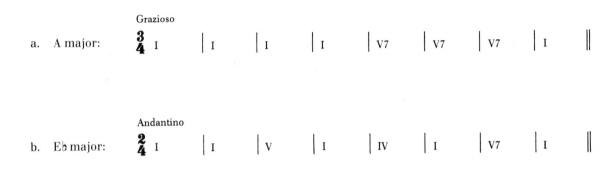

9. Compose a double period for an instrumental combination available in class, employing the period, phrase, and cadence structure outlined here. (Refer to Part V, Unit 23, for information on instrumental ranges and transpositions.)

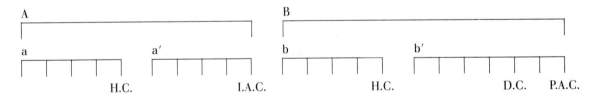

4 The Neapolitan Triad

C: N♭5   N♭6♭3   c: N   N♭6

I. The *Neapolitan triad* is a major triad built on the lowered second scale-degree. Note that in the major mode two alterations are required and in the minor mode, only one. Since the chord frequently occurs in first inversion, it is often spoken of as a *Neapolitan sixth chord* (analyzed N6).

II. The chord has the same function as a diatonic ii chord and most often occurs preceding a cadence. The third is most commonly doubled, and the root and fifth tend to move down to tones of V or V7. The doubled third may remain stationary and become the seventh of V7.

C: I6   N♭6♭3   V   I   c: VI   N♭6   V7♮   i

E: IV   N♭6♭3   cad.[I6♮]   V7   I   e: i6   N♭6   V2/N   N♭6   cad.[i6♮]   V7♯

III. Other uses of the N6 chord follow:

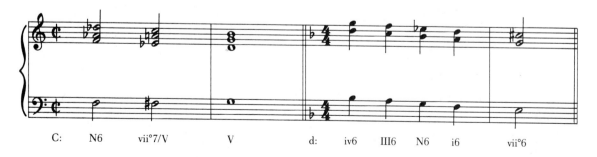

C: N6   vii°7/V   V   d: iv6   III6   N6   i6   vii°6

ant.

e: i6 [n.c. N6] i6 vii°⁶ V⁷♯ i

IV. The N or N6 chord may be used for modulation to both closely and distantly related keys.

    A. The N chord in key 1 becomes any diatonic major triad in key 2.

    B. Any diatonic major triad in key 1 becomes the N chord in key 2.

D: N =   E♭: I A♭:V   E♭: I A♭:V   = D: N
          B♭: IV g: VI   B♭: IV g: VI

f: i   V⁷♮   i   VI   [f: VI6 c: N6]   V⁷♮   i

c: i   vii°⁶   i6   [c: N♭6 A♭: IV♭6] V♭⁶₅   I

Analysis

Analyze music assigned by the instructor. Refer to the Checklist for Analysis (Part V, Unit 21).

Exercises

1. Realize the following figured basses:

   a.

   b.

   c.

2. Harmonize the following melodies, using Neapolitan triads where appropriate. Analyze completely.

   a.

   b.

   c.

3. The following excerpt is from a Vivaldi concerto for violin and organ. Complete the realization of the figured bass in the indicated texture. Then, using the same bass line and chords as a basis, write an original violin line, using Vivaldi as a model. Analyze all work completely.

4. The following patterns may be used for composition or improvisation:

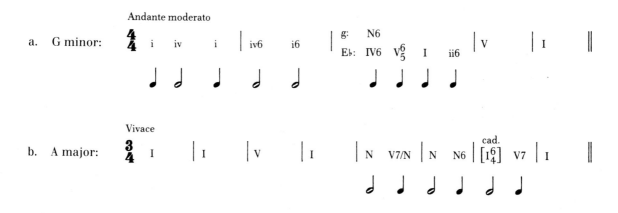

a. G minor:

Andante moderato

4/4 i   iv   i | iv6   i6 | g: N6 / E♭: IV6 V$_5^6$ I ii6 | V | I ‖

b. A major:

Vivace

3/4 I | I | V | I | N V7/N | N N6 | [I$_4^6$] (cad.) V7 | I ‖

5. Compose a phrase group for an instrumental combination available in class, employing the cadence structure outlined here.

a
I.A.C.

b
H.C.

c
P.A.C.

5 Augmented Sixth Chords

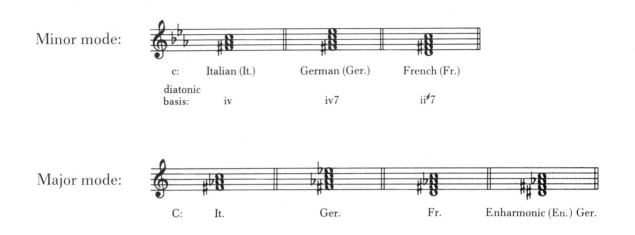

Minor mode:

c: Italian (It.) German (Ger.) French (Fr.)
diatonic
basis: iv iv7 ii⌀7

Major mode:

C: It. Ger. Fr. Enharmonic (En.) Ger.

I. *Augmented sixth chords* are chords containing the interval of the augmented sixth (A6). The four augmented sixth chords are all altered chords. They most often function as dominant preparations, especially at cadential points, and can be used to replace IV, ii, or secondary dominants of V.

II. Each augmented sixth chord contains raised fourth and lowered sixth scale-degrees, both surrounding and tending toward the dominant note. In both modes an accidental is required to raise the fourth scale-degree; in the major mode an accidental also is needed to lower the sixth scale-degree. Note further that the German chord requires a lowered third scale-degree in major and the Enharmonic German, a raised second scale-degree.

III. The augmented sixth chords are shown in the following example in their most common position, with the sixth scale-degree in the bass. Note the three common tones between all four chords and the augmented sixth interval between the bass and tenor voices, which gives rise to the chord's name. Note the doubled tonic scale-degree (the fifth of the chord) in the Italian chord. The Enharmonic German chord is sometimes called the *chord of the doubly augmented fourth* (from A flat to D sharp in this example):

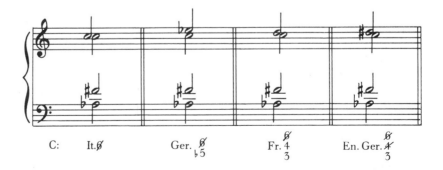

C: It.⌀ Ger. ⌀♭5 Fr. ⌀43 En. Ger. ⌀43

IV. Augmented sixth chords are similar to, and function like, secondary dominants of V. Note the doubled tonic scale-degree in the Italian chord.

C: vii°⁶̸/V   V   It.⁶̸   V   vii°⁶̸♭5/V   V   Ger.⁶̸♭5   V

C: V⁶̸4/V   V   Fr.⁶̸4   V
             3   3

V. The augmented sixth chords usually resolve to V, V7, or I⁶4. The A6 resolves outward by step to a P8 or P15, and the other tones usually resolve by step. Composers sometimes accept the parallel fifths arising when the German chord resolves to V, but see paragraph VI, below.

c: It.⁶̸   V♮   It.⁶̸   [i⁶4]   Ger.⁶̸5   V♮   Ger.⁶̸5   [i⁶4]   C: En.Ger.⁶̸4   [I⁶4]
                                                                                              3

Fr.⁶̸4   V♮   Fr.⁶̸4   [i⁶4]
   3   3

Inversions do not affect resolving tendencies.

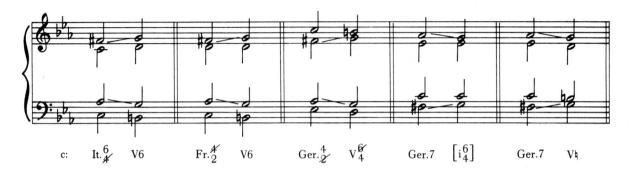

c: It.$\frac{6}{4}$ V6   Fr.$\frac{4}{2}$ V6   Ger.$\frac{4}{2}$ V$\frac{6}{4}$ Ger.7 $\left[i\frac{6}{4}\right]$ Ger.7   V♮

VI. To avoid the parallel fifths resulting from the resolution of the German sixth to V, composers often change the German chord to an Italian or French chord before its resolution. Note the scale-degree changes which result in the alteration of one augmented sixth into another.

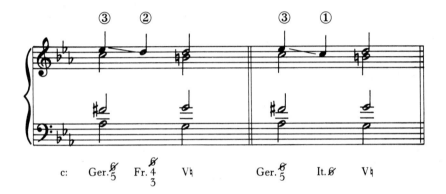

c: Ger.$\frac{6}{5}$ Fr.$\frac{6}{4}$ V♮   Ger.$\frac{6}{5}$ It.$\frac{6}{}$ V♮

When the augmented sixth chords resolve to V7 rather than V, the raised fourth scale-degree often resolves downward (rather than upward, as usual) by a half step to form the seventh of the V7.

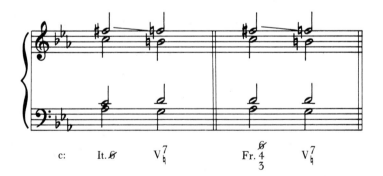

c: It.$\frac{6}{}$ V$\frac{7}{♮}$ Fr.$\frac{6}{4}$ V$\frac{7}{♮}$

VII. Other uses of augmented sixth chords.

    A. Augmented sixth chords may be used as dominant function chords resolving to the tonic triad. In this case they are best analyzed as V7 with a lowered chord fifth (V7♭5) or as vii°7 with a lowered chord third (vii°7♭3). These most often occur with the second scale-degree in the bass (causing a V$\frac{4}{3}$ or vii°$\frac{6}{5}$ position).

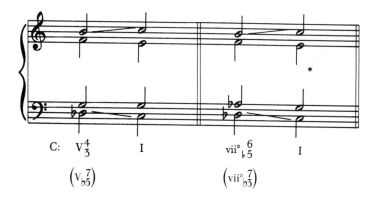

$$\text{C:} \quad V_3^4 \quad\quad I \quad\quad\quad vii°{}_{\flat}{}^6{}_5 \quad\quad I$$

$$\left(V_{\flat5}^7\right) \quad\quad\quad \left(vii°_{\flat3}^7\right)$$

B. Augmented sixth chords may be used as secondary dominant preparation chords, leading to secondary dominants.

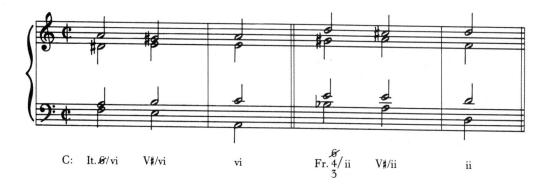

$$\text{C:} \quad \text{It.}\cancel{6}/vi \quad V\sharp/vi \quad\quad vi \quad\quad \text{Fr.}\overset{\cancel{6}}{4}/ii \quad V\sharp/ii \quad\quad ii$$

C. Augmented sixth chords may be used as linear chords, treated as neighbors or appoggiaturas. Compare these chords to the linear diminished seventh chords illustrated in Part III, Unit 3.

Note in the following examples that two voices surround the fifth of the chord being ornamented, and resolve by half step into that note.

$$\text{c:} \quad i \quad \begin{bmatrix}\text{n.c.}\\\text{Ger.}\end{bmatrix} \quad i \quad\quad \text{c:} \quad i6 \quad \begin{bmatrix}\text{n.c.}\\\text{Ger.}\end{bmatrix} \quad i6 \quad\quad \text{c:} \quad i \quad \begin{bmatrix}\text{app.}\\\text{Ger.}\end{bmatrix} \quad i$$

---

*As in the resolution of Ger.⁶₃–V, composers often accept these parallel fifths.

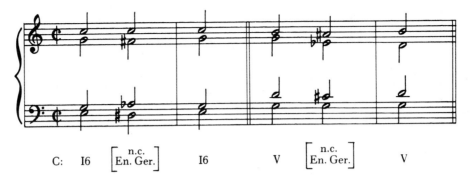

C: I6   [n.c. En. Ger.]   I6   V   [n.c. En. Ger.]   V

D. Augmented sixth chords may be used as modulatory devices. See Part III, Unit 6.

Analysis

Analyze music assigned by the instructor. Be aware, as always, of such elements as motive, line, rhythmic structure, texture, and formal processes. In addition, consider the following:

1. Does the harmonic vocabulary contain augmented sixth chords?

2. Which types are they?

3. Where are they placed in the phrase?

4. How are they related to the chords immediately preceding and following them?

Exercises

1. Spell the Italian, German, and French chords in the following keys, using signatures. For major keys, include the En. Ger: G, B♭, F, A, g, f.

2. Analyze the given augmented sixth chords and resolve as indicated.

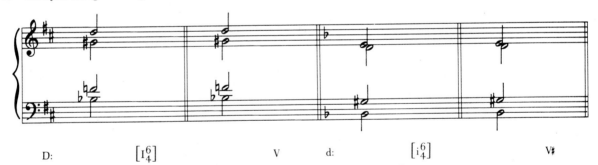

D: [I⁶₄]   V   d: [i⁶₄]   V♯

3. Analyze and resolve the following chords:

e:

4. Harmonize the following melodies and realize the figured and unfigured basses, using augmented sixth chords as indicated by asterisks. Work for strong outer voices and smooth voice leading. Analyze all work fully.

5. Complete the following progressions, employing variant uses of augmented sixth chords as indicated:

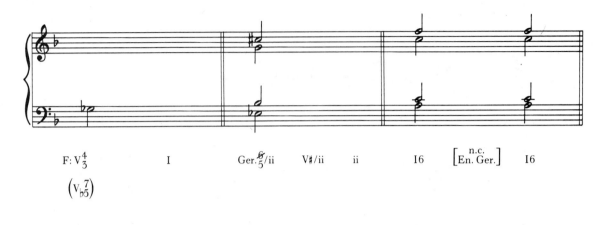

F: V$^4_3$ I   Ger.$^6_5$/ii   V$^\sharp$/ii   ii   I6 $\left[\begin{array}{c}\text{n.c.}\\ \text{En. Ger.}\end{array}\right]$ I6

$\left(V^7_{\flat5}\right)$

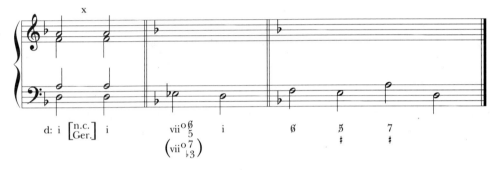

d: i $\left[\begin{array}{c}\text{n.c.}\\ \text{Ger.}\end{array}\right]$ i   vii°$^6_5$ i $\overset{6}{}$ $\overset{5}{\sharp}$ $\overset{7}{\sharp}$

$\left(\text{vii}°^7_{\flat3}\right)$

6. The following patterns may be used for composition or improvisation using various textures and instruments as suggested by the instructor:

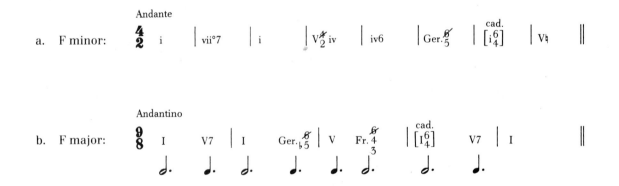

a. F minor: Andante $\frac{4}{2}$ i | vii°7 | i | V$^\sharp_2$ iv | iv6 | Ger.$^6_5$ | $\overset{\text{cad.}}{\left[\text{i}^6_4\right]}$ | V$\natural$ ‖

b. F major: Andantino $\frac{9}{8}$ I | V7 | I | Ger.$_\flat$$^6_5$ | V | Fr.$^6_{4\atop3}$ | $\overset{\text{cad.}}{\left[\text{I}^6_4\right]}$ | V7 | I ‖

7. Compose a theme and at least three variations for instruments available in class. The theme should be a simple binary form, and the harmonic language should reflect that studied so far. Analyze completely.

6 Modulation by Other Means

The following are devices that may be used to modulate between both closely and distantly related keys.

I. Any fully diminished seventh chord can be heard as belonging to several different keys and may be respelled to resolve in any of those keys; thus this chord is useful in modulation. The enharmonically respelled chords may function as dominants, secondary dominants, or linear chords in either or both keys. Furthermore, any member of a diminished seventh chord may be lowered a minor second to change that chord to a dominant seventh.

A. Modulation to closely related keys.

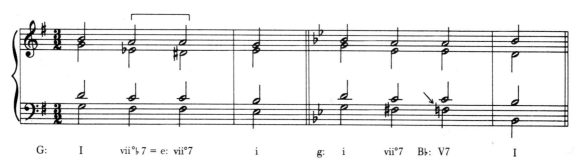

B. Modulation to distantly related keys.

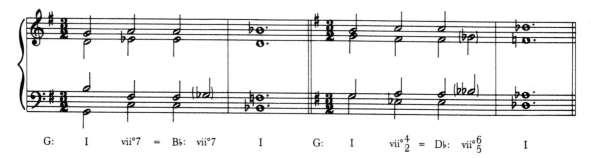

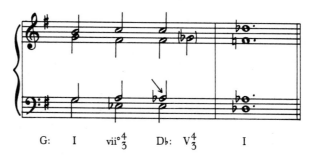

II. The German augmented sixth chord (and Enharmonic German chord) sounds like a dominant seventh, so it can be approached as one function and left as the other. A respelled German chord may become either V7 or any secondary dominant seventh chord, or any dominant seventh chord may be respelled as a German chord.

A. Ger. $^6_5$ becomes V7.

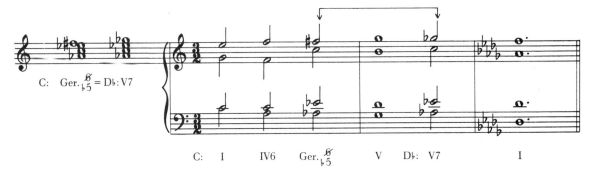

B. V7 becomes Ger. $^6_5$.

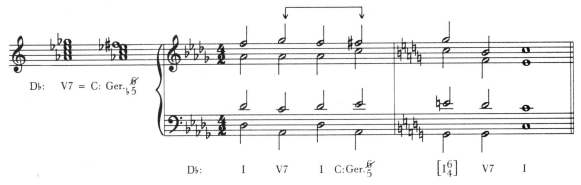

III. In common-tone modulation, a single note common to two keys may be used as a pivot between those keys.

The common note may be enharmonic.

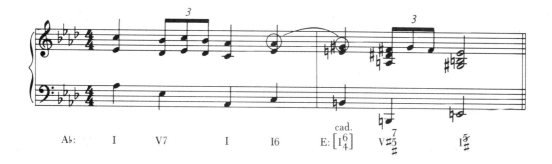

Ab: I   V7   I   I6   E: [I⁶₄cad.]   V⁷♯5♯   I♯5♯

Analysis

Analyze music assigned by the instructor. Consider the following:

1. Where do modulations occur?

2. By what means are they achieved?

3. What keys are involved? What is the intervallic relationship between the tonics?

Exercises

1. Harmonize the following basses and melodies, and analyze:

a.

Eb: V7   D: Ger.⁶₅ [I⁶₄]

b.

g: vii°7 _____ i6   iv6   Bb: vii°7 _____   I

c.

        6   6   6   7   6   7   ⁶₅   6   7   ⁵₃
        5   5   ♭5   4
                                        ♯

d.

Cantabile

vii°7   = B♭:vii°7

e.

2. Write modulating pieces of period length as indicated:

Key 1	Key 2	Method of Modulation
G	f♯	Neapolitan chord
e	G	diminished seventh chord
E♭	G	German chord
E	F	Neapolitan chord
D	E♭	German chord
B♭	A	German chord

3. Discuss choral composition; sing and analyze works from the choral literature. Select a brief text, and compose a short choral setting using materials discussed thus far. Modulate at least once, using one of the means discussed in this unit.

4. Compose a nonperiodic phrase-group for piano or instrumental combination; it should contain modulations by any of the devices discussed thus far.

7 Ninth Chords

g: $V^9_\sharp$ G: V9 V$\flat$9
(Mmm9) (MmM9) or (Mmm9)

I. A *dominant ninth chord (V9)* is a major triad with a minor seventh and a major or minor ninth. With a major ninth, the chord resolves only to a major triad or other seventh chord.

    A. The V9 chord has dominant function and can be used to replace any other dominant function chord except at a half cadence.

    B. Ninth chords are usually found spaced fairly widely, with the ninth always at least a ninth above the root. All inversions are possible, but the fourth inversion is very rare. Figured-bass symbols for inverted ninth chords are unwieldy and are not used in this text. The chord fifth is often omitted. In resolving to I, the ninth resolves down by step, and the other tones resolve as in V7. The ninth often resolves before the rest of the chord, in which case it may be analyzed as a nonharmonic tone. These chords often occur in thicker textures.

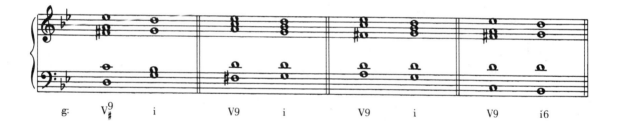

g: $V^9_\sharp$ i V9 i V9 i V9 i6

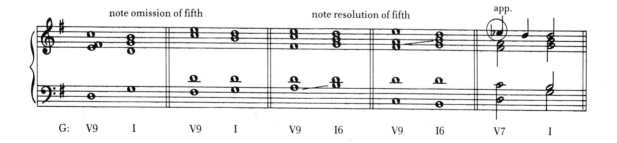

note omission of fifth note resolution of fifth app.

G: V9 I V9 I V9 I6 V9 I6 V7 I

    C. The V7 or V9 chords with raised or lowered chord fifths are found in much late romantic music. For a discussion, refer to Part IV, Unit 4.

II. A *nondominant ninth chord* functions similarly to a nondominant seventh chord and is built over the same scale-degrees. I9, ii9, iii9, iv9, and vi9 are possible. Most nondominant ninths have one of the following qualities: mmM9 or MMM9. Resolution is like that of the dominant ninth, with the chord typically resolving to a seventh chord or another ninth chord.

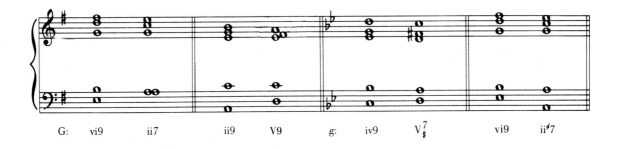

Nondominant or dominant ninth effects may occur over a pedal point, in which case several alternative analyses may be possible.

Analysis

Analyze music assigned by the instructor, keeping in mind all the elements previously considered.

Exercises

1. Resolve the following V9 chords to tonic in root position:

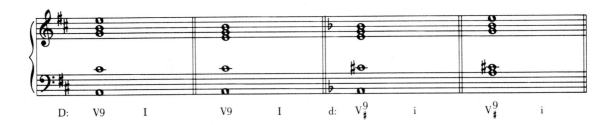

---

*This is read "vi over ii root."

2. Resolve the following nondominant ninth chords as indicated:

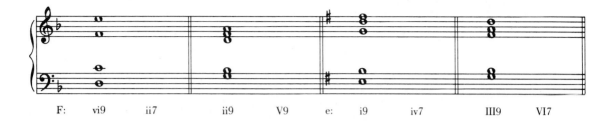

F: vi9   ii7   ii9   V9   e: i9   iv7   III9   VI7

3. Resolve the following inverted V9 chords as indicated:

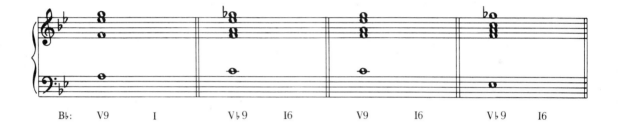

Bb: V9   I   Vb9   I6   V9   I6   Vb9   I6

4. Work out the following melodies and basses, using ninth chords where indicated. Articulate the bass lines in a typical romantic piano texture, and use a fairly full sonority. Analyze fully.

a.

Waltz

G: V9/V   V

b.

9   9   9   9   9 – 8   9 – 8

c.

Adagio

d: V⁷♯   9   i   V⁹♯/iv   iv   V⁹♯/V   V♯

d.

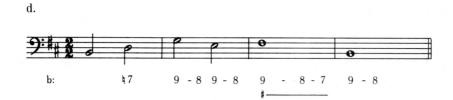

b: ♮7   9 - 8 9 - 8   9 - 8 - 7   9 - 8

5. Select one of the following forms: rounded binary, ternary, or theme and variations. Write an instrumental work for resources available in class, or study text-setting and write an extended choral work or solo song with piano or instrumental accompaniment. The harmonic vocabulary should represent the materials and techniques covered thus far. Refer to the Composition Checklist (Part V, Unit 22).

Part IV

Twentieth-Century
Materials

1 Twentieth-Century Techniques: General Comments

I. The specific *details* of traditional part-writing apply less strictly to twentieth-century music, but the underlying *principles* are the same.

   A. Parallelism of all types of intervals, including perfect fifths, is common, but the principle of linear independence is often the same as in tonal music.

   B. Chords may be built of intervals other than thirds, but the general considerations of good-sounding spacing still apply.

   C. Chords may be highly dissonant, but the necessity for harmonic and textural consistency still applies. The concepts of consonance and dissonance are not necessarily the same as for older music, nor are they necessarily consistent between given twentieth-century works. Each work typically establishes its own norms of consonance and dissonance.

II. Any given piece of twentieth-century music may involve several of the techniques and materials under discussion in the following pages. Few works clearly exemplify only one technique. However, certain techniques and devices tend to be mutually exclusive (for example, modality and serialism).

III. Much twentieth-century music is clearly built around a central tone but lacks the harmonic functions associated with traditional tonality. This music is frequently referred to as *centric*. The use of key signatures is optional and depends on the composer, even with centric music.

IV. Certain techniques or styles of twentieth-century music typically start with only a limited number of pitches (for example, pentatonic or modal music), whereas others regularly use all twelve notes of the chromatic scale. The former tend to be predominantly diatonic, with chromaticism used for variety or increased intensity; the latter tend toward more complex harmonic relationships and a higher dissonance level.

V. *Planing* (pronounced with a long *a*) is a technique involving parallelism of lines or chords. There are two types: chromatic (exact, real) planing, in which the chord structure or harmonic interval is preserved exactly from sound to sound; and diatonic (tonal) planing, where because of the presence of a particular scale, slightly different chords or intervals in successive sonorities may result. Diatonic planing usually supports a feeling of key and scale, whereas chromatic planing does not.

   A. Chromatic planing.

   B. Diatonic planing.

VI. According to the *transposition factor*, any collection of notes will contain certain intervals. If any interval, including inversional equivalents (for example, M2 = m7), is missing in the set, the collection may be transposed by that interval to yield an entirely new collection of notes. Other transpositions will yield one or more notes in common with the original collection. Compositional use can be made of these facts in terms of achieving variety while still using a restricted set of intervals.

Basic collection, lacking m2 (= M7) and A4 (= d5).

Transpositions by m2 and A4 (no common notes with basic collection).

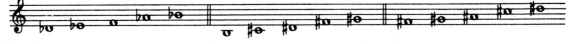

2 Further Concepts for Analysis

Note: Octave doublings and spacings are not taken into account in the following analytic systems.

I. Additional systems.

A. Popular music (jazz) lead sheet symbols.

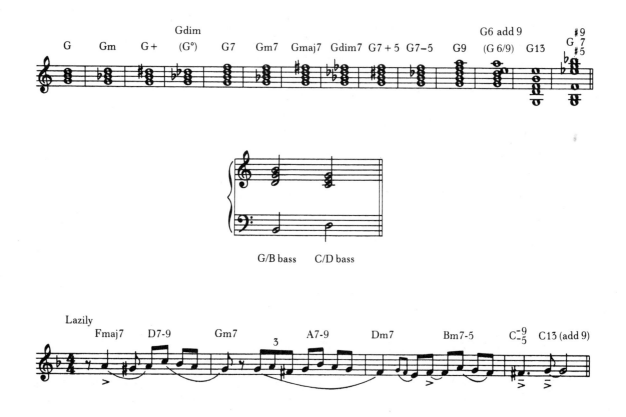

Chord symbols are not standardized, and students are apt to encounter variations of those given above, especially in manuscript arrangements.

B. Because of the complexity of many contemporary chord structures, neither roman numerals nor chord symbols are satisfactory for analysis. For this reason, a number of alternate systems have been devised. These systems have in common the analysis of a group of associated pitches (for instance, a chord, scale, or melodic line) by the quality and number of its constituent intervals. In addition, the Hindemith system seeks to identify a chord root. This root will be the one note that appears as the root of the strongest interval(s) found within the chord.

1. Hanson system:
   p = perfect intervals
   m = major thirds and minor sixths
   n = minor thirds and major sixths
   s = minor sevenths and major seconds
   d = major sevenths and minor seconds
   t = tritones

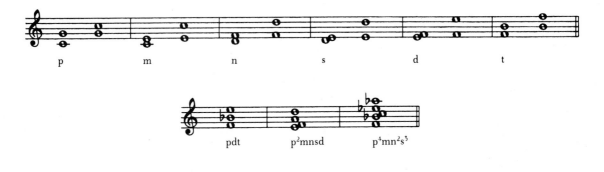

2. Persichetti system:
   (= consonances (Hanson's p, m, n)
   [= mild dissonances (Hanson's s)
   < = sharp dissonances (Hanson's d)
   ⁞ = neutral dissonances (Hanson's t)

3. Hindemith system of root designation.*

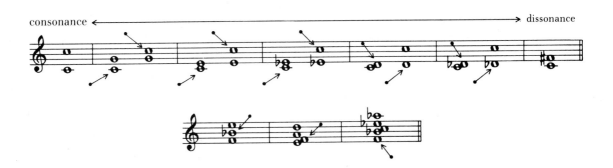

4. Allen Forte, Joel Lester, and many others have developed a method for analyzing atonal and serial music. *Pitch- and interval-class theory* (related to mathematical set theory) in effect also reduces a

—————
*Hindemith derives this concept from the overtone series (see Part V, Unit 2).

complex of notes into its constituent intervals and, much like the Hanson system, enumerates the intervals according to type. In the first example below, the numbers within the brackets indicate that there is one m2 or M7, one P4 or P5, one TT, and no other intervals.

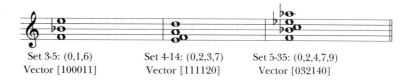

Set 3-5: (0,1,6)   Set 4-14: (0,2,3,7)   Set 5-35: (0,2,4,7,9)
Vector [100011]   Vector [111120]   Vector [032140]

It is beyond the scope of this book to deal with any of these systems in detail. For further information, please consult the references in the following units. The standard books dealing with these systems are all listed in the Bibliography.

II. In addition to the usual items covered in analysis, with twentieth-century music, the following questions should also be considered:

  A. Is the music centric? If so, how is the tonal center established?

  B. What scalar material is used?

  C. What harmonic materials are used? Is there a sense of harmonic progression? If so, how is it controlled? What is the normative dissonance level? How is it established and controlled?

  D. What cadential idioms and devices are employed?

  E. What rhythmic and metric devices are used?

III. Suggested reading (see the Bibliography): Hanson, Hindemith, Persichetti, Forte.†

---

†Supplementary readings are suggested at the end of most units in Part IV; these books are listed in the Bibliography. The student will also find that reference to the various anthologies listed there, as well as to such collections as the *Mikrokosmos* of Bartók, is essential.

3   Rhythmic and Metric Devices

Perhaps the most characteristically original aspect of twentieth-century music is its rhythm. The various devices used are in marked contrast with the metric regularity of common practice music with its functional rhythmic patterns (for example, march or dance) and regular four-bar phrases. Twentieth-century music is often asymmetric; it has complex rhythmic/metric patterns and occasionally gives the effect of unpredictability or great freedom. In certain styles meters are simply omitted; this music is termed *ametrical*.

I. *Irregular meters* are those whose upper numbers are not divisible by 2 or 3 (for example, 5, 7, 11, and 13). The accents fall in alternate two- and three-beat groups.

A. Irregular meters may be simple or compound: $\frac{5}{4}$ or $\frac{15}{8}$. *Composite meters* such as $\frac{5}{8}$ and $\frac{7}{8}$ are irregular meters that represent alternate simple and compound beats, with the value of the eighth note remaining constant. The patterns of twos and threes may remain the same throughout or vary from measure to measure.

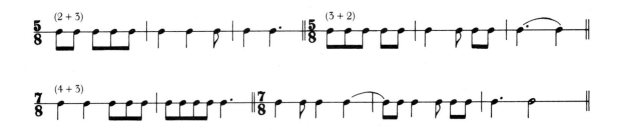

B. An even number of notes can also be organized in composite patterns.

II. In *changing (mixed) meters*, the variables are the number of different meters involved, the number of beats in each meter, and the basic note values of each meter. When two meters having the same unit of beat alternate, the effect is of a composite meter.

172

A. Meters having different lower numbers may alternate. In such cases, one common note value will generally remain constant, and the effect will again be that of a composite meter.

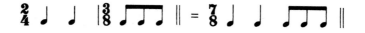

B. Larger patterns of recurring meters are also possible. Meters employing varying numbers and units of beats may be freely intermixed.

C. Effects similar to those previously illustrated may be achieved by using accent marks to displace the normal metric accents.

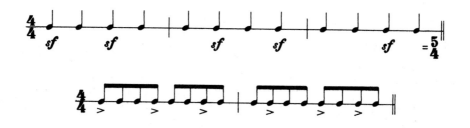

III. Jazz syncopation typically involves a displacement within a regular meter by use of the tie into the strong beat.

IV. Complex rhythmic effects can be achieved by juxtaposing varying rhythmic divisions but keeping a common measure *(polyrhythms)*.

This effect can also be achieved by juxtaposing different metric patterns, keeping a common note value *(polymeters)*.

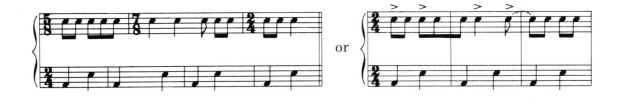

or

Isorhythmic effects involve recurring rhythmic patterns (rhythmic ostinatos) that do not necessarily coincide with pitch patterns.

V. Ametrical rhythmic effects are best notated without a meter signature and without bar lines.

VI. Suggestions for class discussions.

    A. Bring examples from the literature into class.

B. Analyze examples that use many changes of meter.
   1. Is there an overall pattern of repetition?
   2. What relationship exists between the metric patterns and the phrase structure?
   3. What determines the choice of a particular meter?

C. Suggested reading (see the Bibliography): Dallin, Persichetti, Delone.

Exercises

1. Write brief excerpts for unpitched percussion instruments characterized as follows:

   a. In an irregular (composite) meter.

   b. Using extensive meter changes.

   c. Using accent marks to displace the normal metric accent.

2. Write a piece for percussion ensemble, employing polyrhythms and polymeters.

4 Tertian Harmony

I. Traditional *tertian chords* (chords built of thirds) persist into the twentieth century.

    A. Composers use triads of all qualities, including *"indeterminate" triads* (in a tertian context, chords with omitted thirds):

                C   Cm   C+   F#°

    B. "Tall" chords are built by superimposing (stacking) major and minor thirds. The following types of chords are possible.

      1. Traditional sevenths and ninths, either dominant or nondominant.

          Dm9   Fmaj9   F9   Dm9 − 5   Em9 + 7

      2. "Taller" chords constructed by adding thirds beyond the ninth to form dominant or nondominant elevenths or thirteenths.

        Dm9(+ 11) Dm13(+ 11) D9(+ 11) D13(+ 11)

These chords are found most often in root position, with the wider spacings toward the bottom. The uppermost members of the chord (ninth, eleventh, thirteenth, etc.) typically occur in the highest voices. The fifth, and occasionally the third, may be omitted. Very close spacing of these chords, which emphasizes seconds, yields a clusterlike effect. (See Part IV, Unit 8.)

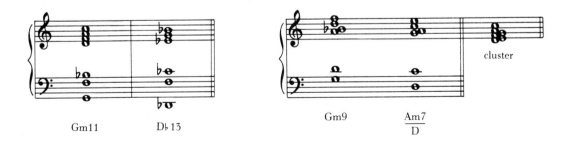

        Gm11   Db 13   Gm9   Am7/D

C. Some of the most common chords are altered dominants. These include ninths and elevenths with raised and/or lowered fifths, and V7 or V9 with both major and minor thirds (often spelled as a raised ninth).

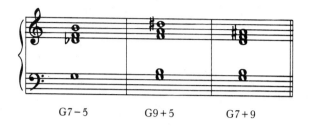

G7 − 5   G9 + 5   G7 + 9

D. *Superposed chords* and *suspensive chords* are similar to tall chords or added note chords with omitted tones; compare them to polychords.

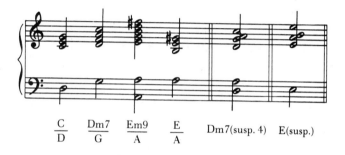

$\dfrac{C}{D}$ $\dfrac{Dm7}{G}$ $\dfrac{Em9}{A}$ $\dfrac{E}{A}$ Dm7(susp. 4)   E(susp.)

E. *Added note chords* are most frequently those with an M2 (or M9) or an M6 above the root of a major or minor triad.

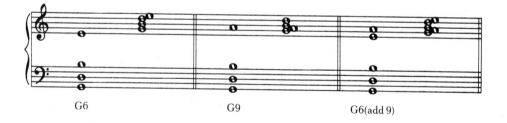

G6   G9   G6(add 9)

The presence of the seventh in an added note chord may result in the sound of a tall chord.

G^{13}_{9}

II. Chord relationships

A. In "functional" root relationships, triads and tall chords may progress quasi-functionally, with root relationships of a fourth and fifth. This is particularly true of altered dominants, which tend to progress around the circle of fifths. Tall chords are now found with "tonic" function. Sevenths and ninths are no longer necessarily considered linear dissonances requiring resolution.

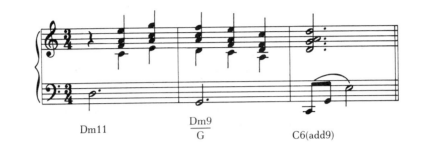

B. In "nonfunctional" root relationships, chords may be associated without reference to traditional tonality. Roots typically move by seconds and thirds. Abrupt modulations and juxtapositions of remote key areas are often the result.

A   Fm   D   E   Dm6   E   Gm

III. Suggestions for class discussion.

   A. Bring examples from the literature into class.

   B. Suggested reading (see the Bibliography): Dallin, Persichetti, Ulehla.

Exercises

1. Compose a brief work for piano, employing dominant and nondominant tall chords in an essentially nonfunctional context. Include some examples of chromatic planing.

2. Compose a passage for string quintet based on the following progression: I–V7/vi–V9/ii–V9/V–V9–vi9–ii9–V9–I. Alter several of the chords as discussed in paragraph II.

3. Write a brief passage in a "cocktail piano" idiom employing planed nondominant tall chords and altered dominant elevenths and thirteenths.

4. Analyze the harmonic structures of the given material, and then complete, using the same vocabulary.

   a.

   b.

   c.

5. Harmonize the following melody, using only triads and seventh chords. Experiment with planing and remote root relationships. Try to avoid common practice clichés.

Al - le - lu - ia   Al - le - lu - ia   Al - le -
lu - ia   Al - le - lu - ia   Al - le - lu - ia   Al - le - lu -
ia   Al - le - lu - ia   Al - le - lu - ia

6. Add an accompaniment to the following tune in "wrong note" style:

Tempo di gavotte

7. The following pattern may be used for composition or improvisation in a jazz or popular idiom:

Bright

F major:	¢ Fmaj7	Fmaj7	Fm7	B♭9	E♭maj7	
	E♭maj7	E♭m7	A♭9	D♭maj7	B♭m B♭m6	
	F6/C bass	D7−9	Dm7/G bass	G♭$^{\#11}_{9}$	Fmaj7	Fmaj7 ‖

5 The Diatonic (Church) Modes

I. The *diatonic (church) modes (mode* is the same as *scale)* follow in the standard terminology in their untransposed (white note) forms. The Ionian mode is not shown, since it is the equivalent of the major scale. The distinguishing intervals of each mode are bracketed.

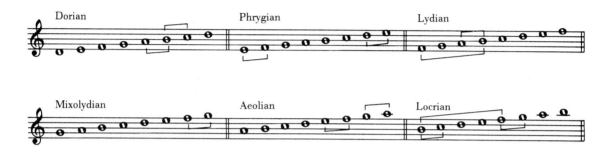

II. The modes are defined by tonic (final), scale-degree relationships, and certain typical melodic cadence formulas.

   A. The Dorian, Phrygian, and Aeolian are often regarded as minor modes. Aeolian has the same structure of interval relationships as natural minor. Dorian is similar to natural minor with a raised sixth scale-degree. Phrygian is similar to natural minor with a lowered second scale-degree. The tonic triads of these modes are minor.

   B. The Lydian and Mixolydian are often regarded as major modes. Lydian is similar to major with a raised fourth scale-degree. Mixolydian is similar to major with a lowered seventh scale-degree. The tonic triads of these modes are major.

   C. The Locrian has a diminished tonic triad and is used less than the other modes.

   D. Some typical cadence formulas follow:

III. Characteristic treatment.

   A. Accidentals should be used sparingly so as not to obscure the sense of mode. The last chord of a piece in a minor mode is often major or omits the third of the tonic triad. The tonic must be clearly defined by means of repetition, return, and emphasis in line and cadences. The sense of modality is often brought out by emphasis on a strongly characteristic scale-degree.

B. It is possible to change modes over a single tonic or to transpose a mode to a new tonic for variety. Modes may be mixed freely within a given passage (the mixture of Dorian and Aeolian is typical). Two or more modes may be used simultaneously for an effect of polymodality. (See Part IV, Unit 9, for a discussion of polytonality.)

IV. Modes may be transposed to another tonic. One method for determining the key signature for a transposed mode follows.

    A. Determine the relationship of the tonic of the untransposed mode to C.

    B. Determine the note that has the same relationship to the tonic of the transposed mode.

    C. Determine the major key signature for that note.

       Example: Find the key signature of Phrygian mode with F♯ as the tonic.

       E : C   as   F♯ : D   two sharps = major key signature for D

V. *Scale and chord.* Modal music tends toward tertian harmony, often with root progressions that emphasize the characteristic modal degrees. Planing is typical. Pandiatonic techniques can be effective (see Unit 7). Quartal harmony can also be used in modal contexts (see Unit 8).

VI. Suggestions for class discussion.

    A. Bring examples from the literature into class.

    B. Carefully analyze and compare all the modes in terms of interval relationships, both (1) between the tonic and other scale-degrees above it, and (2) between adjacent scale-degrees.

    C. Practice transposing the modes onto various finals, both with and without key signatures (Dorian on G, Lydian on B♭, and so forth).

    D. Suggested reading (see the Bibliography): Dallin, Hindemith, Persichetti, Ulehla.

Exercises

1. Construct three cadences in each mode using a variety of soprano lines, chord formulas, and textures.

2. Compose a brief piece for piano. Start in G Dorian, move to G Phrygian, and then move back to G Dorian.

3. Compose a brief piece for an instrumental combination available in class. Start in C Lydian, move to D Lydian, and then move back to C Lydian.

4. Write piano or instrumental accompaniments for the following Appalachian folk melodies. Keep the accompaniments basically simple, with a moderate to slow harmonic rhythm. Use the texture that seems to best complement the melody.

    a.

b.

Moderately

c.

Rhythmically

5. Harmonize the following melodies, arranging them for combinations of instruments available in class. Employ the harmonic vocabulary and technique associated with modal music.

a.

Animé

b.

Bewegt

c.

Dolce

d.

Frisch

e.

Leggiero

6 Exotic (Artificial, Synthetic) Scales

I. Scale forms other than traditional major, minor, and church modes are known as *exotic, artificial,* or *synthetic scales.* Some are derived from folk music, some come from cultures other than Western, and some are constructed by composers to yield special interval relationships. These scale forms may be built on any pitches. Among the most common scales in these categories are the following:

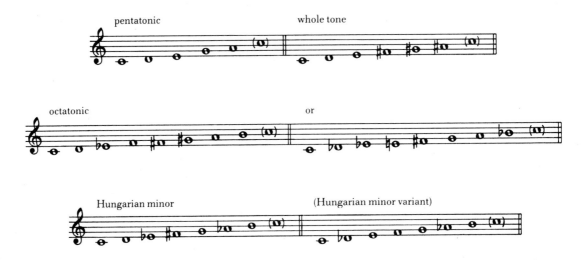

II. Any arrangement of two to twelve notes of the tempered scale may constitute a scale, although most exotic, artificial, and synthetic scales contain five to eight tones. Each scale tends to emphasize certain intervals and may completely lack other intervals. For example, the whole tone scale, rich in M2, M3, and A4 (and their inversions), lacks m2, m3, and P4 (and their inversions). The pentatonic scale lacks m2 and A4. Interval content may affect the choice of transposition. All scales are abstractions; they are merely conventionally arranged collections of notes from which the composer may select in writing music. Composers occasionally employ nonconventional key signatures when exotic or artificial scales are consistently used.

A. In composing with these scales it is important to emphasize the characteristic intervals within each scale, as well as to emphasize clearly the tonic note by the usual means of reiteration, return, line emphasis, and appropriate cadence formulas.

B. Scales often consist of two equivalent *tetrachords* (sets of four adjacent pitches), as in the major scale and the octatonic and Hungarian minor variant. As with the modes, it is possible to change scales over a single tonic or to transpose a scale to a new tonic for variety. Scales may be mixed freely within a given passage or used simultaneously. Frequently the tetrachords may be extracted and used independently.

C. The transposition factor applies to composition with exotic scales. Refer to Part IV, Unit 1, for an explanation and examples.

III. *Scale and chord.* Exotic scales will frequently generate particular types of chord structures.

    A. A pentatonic scale projected as a chord will result in either an additive chord or a quartal (or quintal) stack.

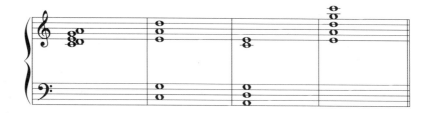

    B. The whole tone scale will generate (1) augmented triads, (2) altered dominants (whole-tone dominants), and (3) clusters.

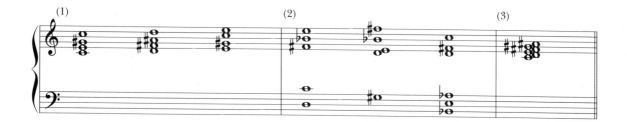

C. The octatonic scale is rich in triads, dominant seventh chords, diminished seventh chords, and poly-chordal combinations (see Unit 9).

IV. Suggestions for class discussion.

   A. Bring examples from the literature into class.

   B. Analyze the interval content of pentatonic, octatonic, and whole tone scales. Which intervals are present? Which are missing? Which transpositions will introduce an entirely new set of notes? Which other trans-positions will introduce certain notes in common with the original scale? How can these facts be used to create musical interest?

   C. Suggested reading (see the Bibliography): Dallin, Hanson, Persichetti, Ulehla.

Exercises

1. Construct five artificial scales consisting of five to nine tones that emphasize certain intervals and avoid others.

2. Compose a brief work for instruments available in class based on one of the scales from Exercise 1.

3. Employing the scale demonstrated in II–A, write a brief work for piano.

4. Write accompaniments for the following pentatonic melodies. Experiment with different harmonic structures and different textures. Try using melodic or chordal ostinatos. Also consider harmonizing the melodies with tones restricted to the tones of the pentatonic scale. Analyze the resulting chord structures.

c.

d.

5. Determine the scale of the given material, then complete, adding six to eight measures:

a.

b.

c.

7 Pandiatonicism

I. *Pandiatonic* (freely diatonic) *music* uses traditional scalar materials, but in somewhat nontraditional ways. In this technique any note of the prevailing scale—most often simply a major scale or diatonic mode—may be combined with any other notes of that scale if the result is pleasing to the composer. Any kind of chord construction may be used, although tertian sonorities are most typical. Tritone relationships are usually avoided, and chromaticism is minimal. The key is firmly established. The most common types of pandiatonic use follow.

A. The composer may use nontraditional arrangements of scalar notes; chords can be understood as tall chords, added note chords, or suspensive chords.

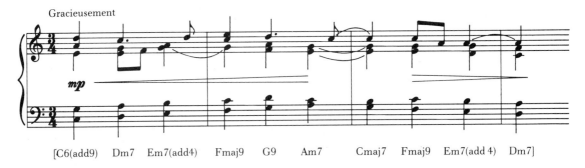

[C6(add9)   Dm7   Em7(add4)   Fmaj9   G9   Am7   Cmaj7   Fmaj9   Em7(add 4)   Dm7]

B. The composer may use tall or additive tertian sonorities, often associated with pedal effects and typically dominant.

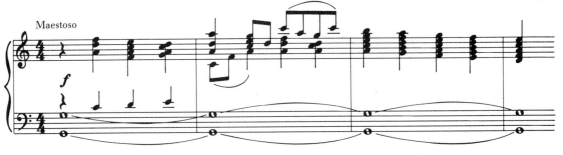

[C: dominant pedal]

C. The composer may use chordal ostinato effects, usually involving alternation of two or three chords.

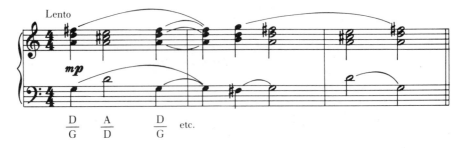

$$\frac{D}{G} \quad \frac{A}{D} \quad \frac{D}{G} \quad \text{etc.}$$

D. The composer may use two contrapuntal "streams" of chords, often resulting in a polychordal sound (see Part IV, Unit 9).

II. Suggestions for class discussion.

    A. Analyze the examples as discussed in paragraph I.

    B. Bring examples from the literature into class.

    C. Suggested reading (see the Bibliography): Dallin, Persichetti, Reti, Ulehla.

Exercises

1. Write six to eight more measures in the style of Example I–A.

2. Write two phrases for piano employing pedal effects as in Example I–B.

3. Continue and complete Example I–D for brass choir.

4. Write a brief choral "Amen," starting as follows:

5. Complete the following fanfare for brass choir:

6. Harmonize the following using a pandiatonic idiom. Strive for an effective accompanimental pattern, possibly an ostinato. Experiment with a variety of devices such as added notes, interior pedal points, and so forth. This may be written for piano or instruments available in class.

8 Quartal and Secondal Harmony

I. Chords may be constructed of intervals other than thirds; fourths, fifths, or seconds are frequently used. Perfect fourths may be superimposed or combined with augmented fourths. Perfect or diminished fifths can also be used.

II. The use of the Hanson, Persichetti, and Hindemith systems is appropriate in the analysis of quartal and secondal harmony. (See Part IV, Unit 2.)

$p^4mn^2s^3$

Hanson   Persichetti   Hindemith

III. Secondal sonorities are often the result of closely spaced quartal or tertian chords. The effect of a sonority results not so much from the intervals it contains as from the spacing of these intervals. Thick secondal sonorities are usually termed *clusters*.

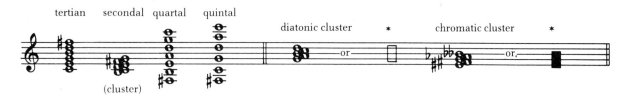

tertian   secondal   quartal   quintal   diatonic cluster   *   chromatic cluster   *

(cluster)

IV. Since traditional chord names do not apply to nontertian harmony, the following terminology is suggested:

Number of Different Notes in a Chord	Name
2	dyad
3	triad (trichord)
4	tetrad
5	pentad
6	hexad
7	heptad

---

*For further examples of nontraditional notation, see Stone.

V. Few works are consistently quartal or secondal. Often the two types can be mixed, and both work well with tertian material, including tall chords. Quartal chords can gain greater variety by inverting the intervals they contain. (The term *inversion* does not apply here in the traditional sense, since the quality and function of quartal materials alter with rearrangement.) A four- and a three-note quartal sonority follow, each followed by chords derived through inversion:

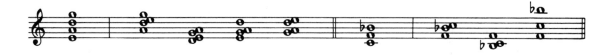

VI. Some possible cadences follow. Note that the first two examples contain chords derived exclusively from perfect fourths. The third example contains both perfect and augmented fourths, and its final chord is a triad.

VII. *Chord and melody.* In quartal context, melodic lines will often reflect the underlying quartal harmony by using frequent leaps of fourths. Projections of fourths and sequential patterns typically result in the use of all the notes of the chromatic scale.

VIII. Suggestions for class discussion.

    A. Bring examples from the literature into class.

    B. Carefully analyze the following sonorities, using any system. (See Part IV, Unit 2, for various systems.)

    C. Suggested reading (see the Bibliography): Dallin, Hanson, Hindemith, Persichetti, Ulehla.

Exercises

    1. Respace and rearrange (by inversion of intervals) each of the following sonorities in at least five ways:

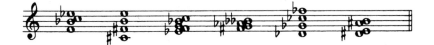

2. Analyze the intervallic content of the given chords, and then complete:

a.

b.

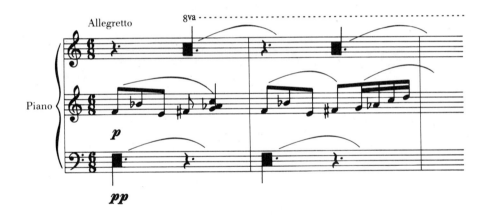

3. Continue the following for ten to fifteen measures:

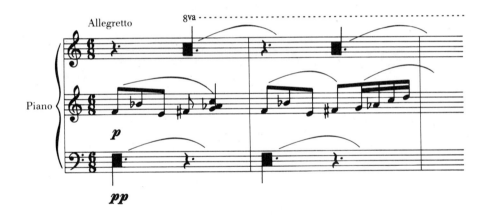

4. Compose a brief work for instruments available in class using nontertian chord structures.

9 Polyharmony and Polytonality

I. *Polyharmony* involves the simultaneous sounding of two or more tertian chords with distinct roots *(polychords)*. The variables are the quality of the chords, the root relationships, and the spacing or arrangement of the chords. Polychords may be used within a diatonic context (Example a) or a chromatic context (Example b). Note the analysis.

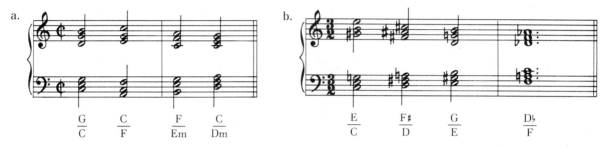

Chords most often used are major, minor, Mm7, and MM7. Roots may all be similarly related, or there may be no system for root selection.

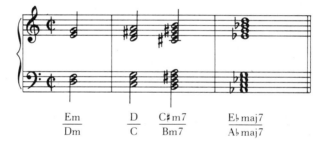

The chords in a polychord are kept distinct by spacing, by placing the chords in contrapuntal "streams," or by contrasting orchestration; otherwise, certain spacings will be ambiguous. For example, is apt to sound like a tall chord, whereas 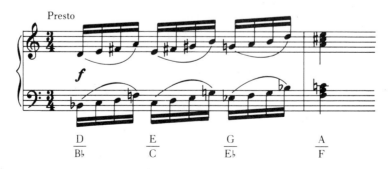 will sound like a cluster.

Polychords may also be expressed in linear fashion:

194   TWENTIETH-CENTURY MATERIALS

II. *Chord and scale.* Diatonic polychords will typically reduce to a simple diatonic scale (major or church mode) and the effect is often like pandiatonicism. Chromatic polychords may reduce to a single exotic scale, frequently octatonic.

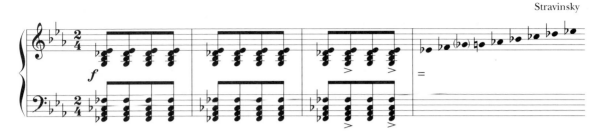

III. *Polytonality* involves the simultaneous sounding of two or more distinct areas of tonality, expressed as lines or chords. The variables are the scale or mode of each element and the relationship of the tonics. Traditional scalar materials are usually used. Each scalar element must be kept distinct by spacing or orchestration.

Tonal areas can be made distinct from one another by selecting keys with the most distant tonal relationships to provide the fewest common notes between scales. Occasionally, however, the composer will choose scales that provide for common tones; the result is very similar to a synthetic scale or a permutational scale, in which certain tones occur in both raised and lowered form.

The following example is both polychordal and polytonal:

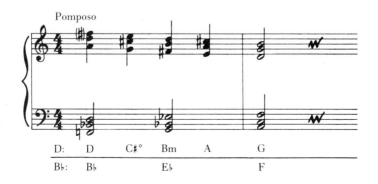

Polytonal passages are usually resolved in one of two ways: into a sonority containing elements of both keys or into a single key. Polytonal material is often used in brief, isolated passages.

IV. Suggestions for class discussion.

   A. Bring examples from the literature into class.

   B. Experiment with polychords, trying major triads in various root relationships and spacings. Also try MM7 and MMM9 chords.

   C. Analyze several polychordal examples. What root relationships are used? Is there a clear rationale for the chord successions and/or root relationships? What qualities of triads seem to work best together?

   D. Suggested reading (see the Bibliography): Dallin, Persichetti, Ulehla.

Exercises

1. Experiment with polytonality. Set up a simple accompaniment pattern, keeping to a single tonal area. Write a melody against it that begins in the same key, moves through distinctly contrasting keys, and then returns to the original key.

2. Write brief passages for piano that illustrate the following:

   a. Diatonic polychords within G major, using nonsystematic root relationships.

   b. Chromatic polychords, using systematic root relationships and/or exact planing.

3. Write a two-voice contrapuntal example using a polyharmonic chordal basis.

4. Write a two-voice example using two modes or synthetic scales having some common tones. If possible, use different key signatures or partial signatures for each voice (in the style of Bartók).

5. Analyze the given material, and complete in the same idiom:

   a.

   b.

6. Continue harmonizing the following melody, employing either diatonic or chromatic polychords:

10 Intervals in Twentieth-Century Music

I. Much contemporary music is conceived in terms of the manipulation of a restricted set of intervals instead of scale-forms, traditional materials, or serial processes. In this procedure a basic interval *cell* (or *set*) may give rise to a whole work, in both its harmonic and linear aspects. The cell itself may be treated as a motive. A cellular approach typifies much serial music (see Part IV, Unit 11). Much music of this type is not strongly centric and is frequently termed *atonal*.

II. Characteristic procedures.

   A. The basic cell, or set of interval relationships, may be altered in any of the following ways:

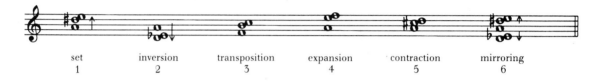

set	inversion	transposition	expansion	contraction	mirroring
1	2	3	4	5	6

   B. The cell is usually applied to both the vertical and horizontal aspects and often accounts for most of the sounds heard in a work. The following excerpt uses the first five of the derivations in the example in II–A.

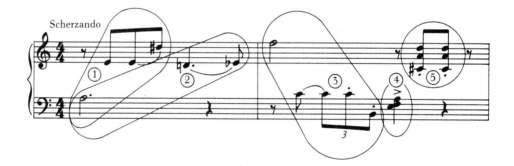

   C. Many interesting chords can be built by projecting two or more different intervals in succession. In such sonorities, note duplication at the octave or fifteenth is usually avoided. Melodic lines may be derived from any of the resultant sonorities.

   M3, m3   P4, A4   P5, M3   (line derived from 3)

III. The transposition factor is especially relevant to interval music. Any set lacking a given interval or its inversion may be transposed by that interval, yielding pitches not contained in the original set.

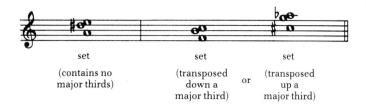

set
(contains no
major thirds)

set
(transposed
down a   or
major third)

set
(transposed
up a
major third)

IV. Suggestions for class discussion.

    A. Bring examples from the literature into class.

    B. Suggested reading (see the Bibliography): Cope, Dallin, Forte, Hanson, Persichetti, Ulehla, Delone.

Exercises

1. Experiment with building massive dissonant sonorities by projecting in alternation two or three different intervals, as suggested in II–C. Analyze the results using the Hanson system or some other method of interval analysis.

2. Build several chords by mirroring around a central note. Analyze according to the instructions for Exercise 1.

3. Compose a brief work for piano based on the interval set G–B♭–C–F♯. Derive both melody and harmony from the set and its transpositions. Try to construct a convincing cadence.

4. Compose a short work for instruments available in class using the basic cell of the example in II–A.

5. Analyze the given material, and continue in the same idiom:

11 Twelve-Tone Serialism

I. Serial procedures can become complex, but the basic principles are simple.

A. In *twelve-tone serialism,* a *tone-row* (set, or *row* for short) of twelve different *pitch-classes** (p.c.'s) is set up to control relationships. Pitches may be sounded in succession (melodically) or simultaneously (harmonically) and may be sounded in any octave. Notes may be repeated directly, but no pitch-class may be reused until the entire row has been sounded. Rows may be broken down into two groups of six notes each (hexachords) or three groups of four notes each (tetrachords). Divisions into three-note groups and even two-note groups are also found.

In serial music, the row will "control" the whole work, in both its harmonic and linear aspects. A single statement of the row may coincide with a phrase, or statements of the row may be independent of formal structure, though row forms and variants or particular transpositions may be used to define contrasting sections of larger movements.

B. Four forms of the row are available: Prime (P_0) or Original (O_0), Inversion (I_0), Retrograde (R_0), and Retrograde Inversion (RI_0).

C. Any of the four basic forms may be transposed, giving a total of forty-eight possible associated sets. The level of transposition is indicated by the small number following the initial designating the form of the row. This number indicates the number of semitones above the reference pitch. Thus P_6 indicates the prime form of the row transposed up a tritone (six semitones higher). The reference pitch for transpositions of P and I forms is the first pitch-class of P_0; the reference pitch for transpositions of R forms is the first pitch-class of R_0; the reference pitch for transpositions of RI forms may be either the first pitch-class of R_0 or the first pitch-class of I_0.

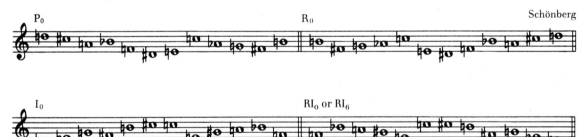

Much serial music employs the convention of using an accidental, including the natural sign, before each note. In this case, the accidental refers *only* to that note, and does not carry through the measure.

---

*Any pitch, regardless of octave, having the same specific letter name belongs to the same pitch-class. For example, all A flats belong to the pitch-class A flat. Enharmonic equivalents are in the same pitch-class; thus, G sharp is in the same pitch-class as A flat.

II. Some principal variation techniques.

A. Any two or more tone row forms may be used simultaneously.

B. The principle of strict succession may be varied by ostinatos, trills, repeated notes, pedal effects, tremolos, or chords.

C. *Segmentation* involves the partitioning of 12 tone sets into *subsets* or *segments*, usually into hexachords (6 p.c.'s) or trichords (3 p.c.'s), which are often used somewhat independently of each other in a given work. Schönberg's technique typically involves independent hexachords; Webern often works with trichords. In a derived set (see the Webern example under III), permutations of the first trichord of a set give rise to the subsequent trichords.

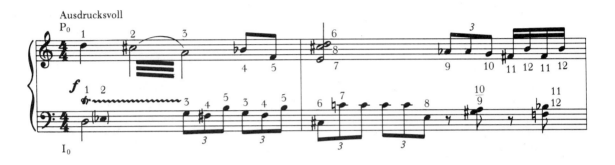

III. A multitude of different rows is possible. The composer constructs or selects a basic row on the basis of the particular interval characteristics it exhibits and selects from the forty-eight forms those few that yield the interval or pitch relationships to be exploited. All forty-eight forms are rarely used in a single work. Most serial music is clearly not strongly centric, but there is no reason why it cannot be. Some rows are very traditional in effect, such as the following Berg example; others (Nono, Webern) are less so.

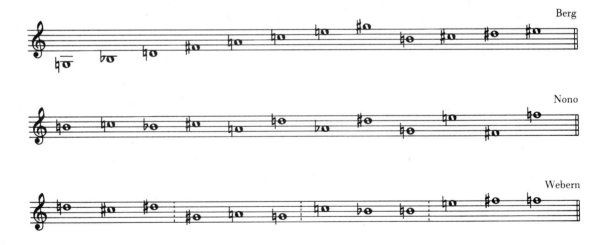

Rows of fewer than twelve notes may be used.

IV. Row forms and transposition levels are determined by a number of considerations. A particular transposition may result in the pitch classes associated with certain intervals remaining the same. These intervals are called *invariants*, and can be of great use in establishing the relationship among row forms, or as a means of unification.

Schönberg Op. 25

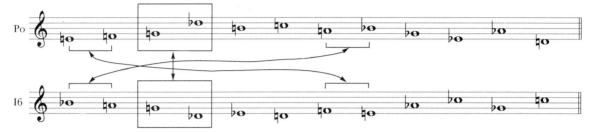

A composer may desire a high degree of invariance, or no invariance at all.

Certain rows are structured in such a way that a specific transposition or permutation of the first hexachord will produce the complementary pitch classes, that is, the pitch classes of the second hexachord. This means that the hexachords of the two row forms can be combined to produce the total chromatic. Rows of this kind are called *combinatorial*. Smaller segments may also be combinatorial. The Webern example cited above is an all-combinatorial row.

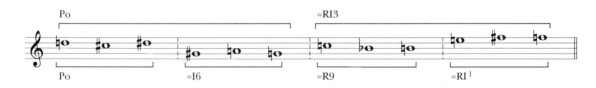

Combinatorality is another factor that composers may use in narrowing the choice of row forms or transpositions from among all the possible row forms available. Like invariants, combinatorial rows provide for greater unity and coherence.

Babbit *Duet*

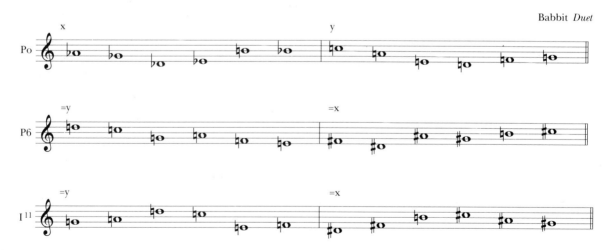

V. In *integral serialism* (total serialism, total organization), elements in addition to pitch are organized in terms of numerical series.

VI. Suggestions for class discussion.

    A. Bring examples from the literature into class.

    B. Analyze all the rows given in III for interval content. Discuss the construction of these rows.

    C. How can the mathematical theory of sets (groups) be used to write or analyze serial music?

    D. Suggested reading (see the Bibliography): Brindle, Cope, Dallin, Forte, Perle, Persichetti, Reti, Ulehla, Delone.

Exercises

1. Write a brief work for piano using only the basic row form (P_0) shown in I–C.

2. Using the three rows illustrated in III, write excerpts for piano. Note the resulting interval relationships, especially the interval content of chords formed from the rows.

3. Write original rows in the following ways:

    a. Construct a row to achieve maximum variety in interval relationships.

    b. Construct a row to achieve minimum variety in interval relationships.

4. Analyze the serial and intervallic structure of the given material, and continue or complete:

    a.

    b.

    c.

Note: Each accidental affects only the note immediately following it.

12 Additional Contemporary Procedures*

I. A degree of chance is inherent in all music; this is caused by the imperfections of notation and performance variables. Baroque music, like much jazz, introduces a number of partially controlled elements (ornamentation, tempo fluctuations, and figured-bass improvisation). All live performance introduces unpredictable elements. Some recent composers have systematically introduced *random (aleatoric) elements* into their music, with some exerting only minimal control over the result and others determining all but a few details.

   A. Indeterminate elements often result from practical considerations. For example, if the composer has in mind only the following generally fast, disjunct fragment that accelerates,

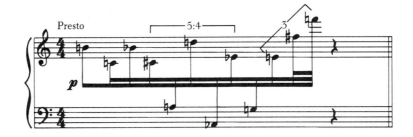

it may be more efficient to notate it in *proportional notation.*

Frame notation can also be used.

---

*For further examples of nontraditional notation, see Stone.

B. The composer may leave the overall form of a work up to the performers, who are given only the details and told to play them in any order. Alternatively, the composer may predetermine the form and leave a few (or many) details somewhat (or very) open.

C. The composer must decide what elements he or she wants to control, how and to what extent they may be controlled, and how to notate the desired effect precisely.

II. In some recent music, called *texture music*, sonority has become the primary compositional consideration. Typically, this music involves clusters of varying density, dynamics, and color, as well as unusual uses of traditional instruments and nontraditional sound sources. Traditional concern with line, pitch, rhythm and meter, and harmonic progression tends to be subordinated or eliminated.

III. *Minimalism* is characterized by severe restriction of materials (pitch, rhythm, color, density, and register). Repetition with slight variations is the main device. The music unfolds through the addition of new strands or layers, as well as rhythmic phase relationships.

IV. Electronic music is a major area of contemporary musical practice that, because of its highly specialized and technical nature, is beyond the framework of this text. Useful studies for the beginning student may be found in the books listed in the Bibliography under Electronic Music.

V. Suggestions for class discussion.

A. Bring examples from the literature into class.

B. Discuss chance elements in traditional music.

C. Discuss the æsthetic implications of chance procedures and minimalism.

D. Analyze examples of texture music and pieces using aleatoric processes. What notational and calligraphic devices are employed? To what degree is traditional notation still employed? What unusual sound resources and techniques are used?

E. Suggested reading (see the Bibliography): Cope, Forte, Nyman, Delone.

Exercises

1. Write a piece for the class to perform using the techniques of minimalism.

2. Write a piece for the class in which the overall form is predetermined and the details left open; then write a piece using the opposite approach.

3. Construct an ensemble piece in which fragments in frame notation can be arbitrarily ordered and combined.

4. Write a piece using proportional notation. Experiment with various means of notating pitches with long durations.

Part V

Reference Materials

1 Musical Calligraphy

Common calligraphic errors (numbers refer to items in the checklist for musical calligraphy):

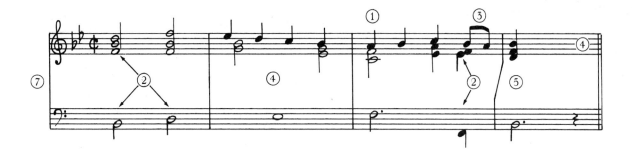

Corrected example:

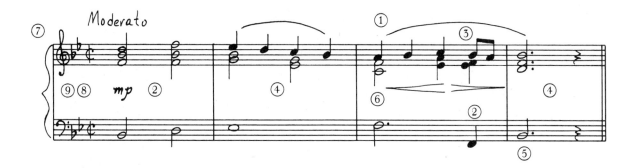

I. Checklist for musical calligraphy.

1. Note heads are filled in where needed and are large enough to fill the space.

2. Stems are vertical, thin, connected to heads and beams, going in proper direction, and on the proper side of the note head.

3. Beams are thick and straight, following the direction of the beamed group.

4. Alignment is perfect within each beat, and beats are evenly distributed in each bar; all beats are accounted for by notes or rests.

5. Bar lines are thick, straight, and vertical; they are laid out beforehand to fill the page.

6. Editing is full and specific; tempo, phrasing, and dynamics are included.

7. A brace is needed for the great staff.

8. The meter signature appears only at the beginning, unless the meter changes during the piece.

9. The clef and key signature must be repeated at the beginning of each staff.

II. Equipment.

    A. Fountain-type pen with a broad nib, special music pen, black felt-tip pen, or soft pencil.

    B. Black ink (for example, Pelikan Fount India or Higgins Eternal).

    C. Good-quality manuscript paper.

    D. Ruler.

    E. Ink eraser or single-edged razor blade.

III. Several good music manuscript manuals are available.

2 The Overtone Series

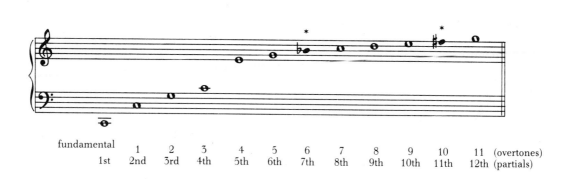

fundamental	1	2	3	4	5	6	7	8	9	10	11	(overtones)
1st	2nd	3rd	4th	5th	6th	7th	8th	9th	10th	11th	12th	(partials)

A vibrating body, such as an air column or string, vibrates not only over its entire available length (producing the fundamental *frequency*, perceived as pitch), but also in fractional parts (one-half of its length, one-third of its length, and so on), which produces *overtones*. These overtones, or *harmonics*, are too weak in volume *(amplitude)* to be heard as individual pitches, but they do contribute to the color *(timbre)* of the sound. The overtones are usually multiples of the frequency of the fundamental, except with very complex sounds. For instance, with a fundamental of 100 vibrations (cycles) per second, the first overtone has 200 cycles per second (sounding one octave higher); the second overtone, 300 cycles per second (sounding a twelfth higher); the third, 400 cycles per second (sounding two octaves higher); and so on.

Note that the fundamental is also termed the *first partial*, resulting in a discrepancy of numbering between overtones and partials.

---

*These tones are significantly out of tune compared to the tempered system.

3 Nonharmonic (Nonchord) Tones

Any note that is not heard as a member of the prevailing harmony (chord) at any given time is defined as a *nonharmonic (nonchord) tone.* In some highly dissonant contemporary styles this concept is inapplicable. The following are the most common types of nonharmonic tones.

I. A *passing tone* (p.t.) is used stepwise to fill in the gaps between chord tones in a line. These may be accented or unaccented. The example in I–C is often analyzed as an appoggiatura, since it is longer than its resolution and appears on a strong beat.

II. An *auxiliary tone* (aux., or *neighbor tone*) is used between a chord tone and its repetition. It may or may not be accented or in pairs, as it is in II–C.

III. An *escape tone* (e.t., or *échappée*) is unaccented, approached by step, and resolved by skip.

IV. A *free neighbor* (f.n., or *incomplete neighbor tone*) is unaccented, approached by skip, and left by step, usually in the opposite direction. It can be thought of as an unaccented appoggiatura.

V. An *anticipation* (ant.) is unaccented, anticipates a chord tone, and is usually shorter than this tone. It is typically a cadential idiom.

VI. A *pedal tone* (ped., or *pedal point*) is of long duration; it is prepared and resolved on the same pitch. A pedal tone is usually on the tonic or dominant note and serves to prolong that harmony through a passage, in which case the other voices sound like decorations of that harmony.

G: V ───   I ─────────────────

VII. An *appoggiatura* (app., or *"leaning note"*) is accented, approached by skip, and resolved by step, usually in the opposite direction. It is often longer than its resolution. The example in VII–C may be analyzed as an accented passing tone.

VIII. A *suspension* (susp.) is accented, prepared by a chord tone on the same pitch, and resolved by step. The suspension figure requires preparation (prep.) on a chord tone, dissonance (diss.) on a relatively strong beat, and resolution (res.) by step to a chord tone. The upward-resolving suspension is sometimes called a *retardation*. The suspension does not have to be tied from its preparation. The arabic numerals (in the following example) are used to classify suspension figures and refer to the interval formed between the bass and the suspending voice on the suspension and resolution beats. The following idioms are common harmonic contexts for the suspension figure:

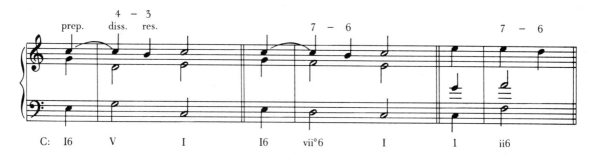

C: I6   V   I   I6   vii°6   I   I   ii6

The resolution may be ornamented (VIII–A), or the chord may be changed at the point of resolution (VIII–B).

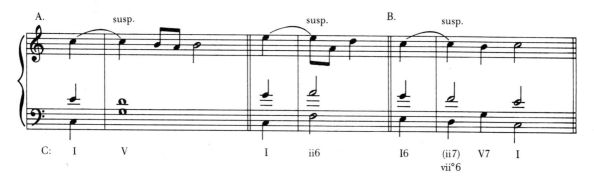

C: I   V   I   ii6   I6   (ii7)   V7   I
                                   vii°6

4 Relative and Linear Motion

I. *Relative motion* is the directional relationship between two voices.

    A. In *similar motion*, voices move in the same direction.

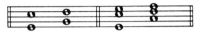

    B. In *contrary motion*, voices move in opposite directions.

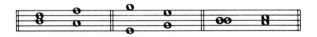

    C. In *oblique motion*, one voice moves while the other remains stationary.

    D. In *parallel motion*, voices move in the same direction by the same interval.

II. *Linear motion* is melodic motion found within a single voice.

    A. In *conjunct motion*, notes move by step.

    B. In *disjunct motion*, notes move by skip.

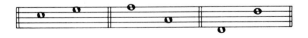

5 Guidelines for Voice Leading in Strict Four-Part Writing

In freer textural and stylistic situations, the following guidelines for voice leading in strict four-part writing may be applied less strictly.

I. Avoid crossing and overlapping voices.

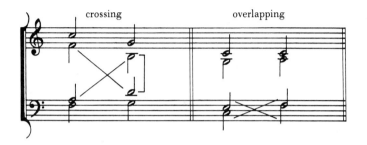

II. Avoid parallel fifths and octaves, as well as octaves or fifths by contrary motion.

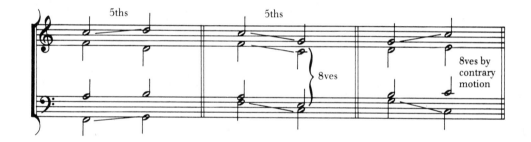

III. Avoid leaps in similar motion to octaves or fifths in the outer voices, except in chord repetition. (These are termed *direct* or *hidden fifths* or *octaves*.)

IV. Do not allow three voices to leap in the same direction unless the fourth voice remains stationary or moves in contrary motion, except in chord repetition. (See the example in III.)

V. Avoid a diminished fifth moving to a perfect fifth in the outer voices (unequal fifths). However, a perfect fifth may move to a diminished fifth if the diminished fifth is subsequently resolved.

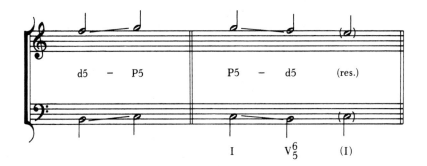

VI. In connecting chords a second apart, both of which are in root position, make the outer voices move in contrary motion. This procedure will also hold true when the bass moves by the interval of a second, as when one of the chords is in inversion, with the exception of consecutive first-inversion chords.

VII. Avoid the augmented second melodically when involved with a change of chord.

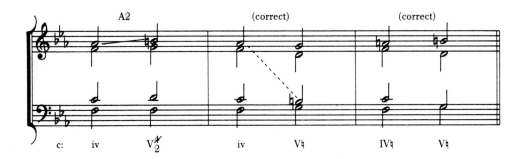

VIII. Avoid the melodic tritone (T) unless properly resolved or part of the same chord.

IX. Strive for basically conjunct motion in the upper voices.

X. Try to maintain consistent spacing within a phrase. Changes in spacing should be made only when warranted by such considerations as a wide leap in the soprano. In that case, the spacing change will allow for smoother voice leading in the interior voices.

6 Guidelines for Doubling in Strict Four-Part Writing

I. Avoid doubling tendency tones (leading tones or chord sevenths).

II. Doubling should clearly establish the function of the chord: roots first, fifths next, and thirds last. Linear considerations always take precedence.

III. Chord fifths occasionally may be omitted. When this occurs the root may be tripled. In the case of four-tone chords, the root may be doubled.

IV. Chord thirds are rarely omitted in predominantly chordal textures.

V. Summary:

Chord	Preference for Doubling
major and minor triads in root position	root, fifth, third
tonic, subdominant, and dominant triads in first inversion	root, fifth, third
supertonic, submediant, and mediant triads in first inversion	third, root, fifth
diminished and augmented triads in root position or first inversion	third, root

VI. Scale-degrees 1, 4, and 5 are most often doubled; 2, 3, and 6, less so; and the leading tone, very rarely.

7 Checklist for Part Writing

Students are urged to check all written work systematically as they write it, both for musicality and technique. All work must be played or sung after completion. Some of the following items apply only at the later stages of study.

I. Play or sing each voice as you write it to check the *line* for the following:

    A. Voices are smooth and directional.

    B. There are no unnecessary large leaps.

    C. There are no unresolved diminished or augmented intervals.

    D. The outer voices have a clear contour (shape).

    E. There is a reasonable range and tessitura.

    F. Idioms are appropriate to the medium.

II. To check *counterpoint*, play each pair of voices, and check for the following:

    A. No parallel fifths or octaves should occur.

    B. No hidden octaves or fifths, or unequal fifths between the outer voices, should occur.

    C. No voice crossing or overlapping.

    D. There should be a good contrapuntal relationship between the outer voices.

III. *Spacing*.

    A. Consistent spacing should exist within each phrase.

    B. No large gaps between upper voices should occur.

    C. The texture should be homogeneous.

IV. *Doubling* should be preponderantly normal, except when factors of line take precedence.

V. *Calligraphy*.

    A. Editing should be complete, when appropriate.

    B. Notation should be clear.

VI. Complete *analysis* includes cadences, chords, nonharmonic tones, and phrase and period structure if appropriate.

8 Chord Functions in Tonal Music

I. In the following common diatonic chord progressions, roman numerals are shown as they occur in the major mode. The root relationships are also valid in the minor mode.

A. Dominant functions: V–I or vii°–I.

B. Dominant preparation: IV–V, ii–V, or vi–V.

C. Roots move downward by fifth (quasi-dominant) relationships: (IV–vii°)–iii–vi–ii–V–I.

D. Roots move downward by thirds: I–vi–IV–ii.

E. Roots move upward by thirds: I–iii.

F. Roots move downward by seconds: vi–V.

G. Roots move upward by seconds: I–ii, iii–IV, IV–V, V–vi, or vii°–I.

Chord Chart   **(in sequence)**

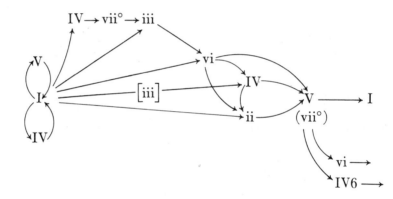

All chords are considered functional and tend to progress in the direction indicated by the arrows.

II. Chord classification system.*

Class	Diatonic Repertoire	Chromatic Repertoire
6	IV†, IV7†	secondary dominants of VII
5	vii°†, vii°7†	secondary dominants of iii
4	iii, iii7	secondary dominants of vi
3	vi, vi7	secondary dominants of ii, IV
2	ii, ii7, IV, IV7	secondary dominants of V, aug. sixths, Neapolitan chords
1	V, V7, vii°, vii°7	V7(♭5), V7(+5)

---

*The classification system suggested here follows that set out by Allen Irvine McHose in *The Contrapuntal Harmonic Technique of the Eighteenth Century* (New York: Appleton, 1947).
†In diatonic sequences only.

A. Types of progression.
   1. *Normal progression* moves downward, class to class (iii–vi, vi–ii, and so forth).
   2. *Retrogression* moves upward by skip or step (ii–vi or ii–iii).
   3. *Elision* moves downward by skip (iii–IV or vi–V).

B. Comments on the classification system.
   1. The fifth and sixth classes are rare.
   2. Chords in the first and second classes and tonic predominate in most tonal styles.
   3. Augmented sixth chords are sometimes found in classes other than second.
   4. Ninth chords may substitute for sevenths in any class.
   5. The tonic chord may normally progress to any other class.
   6. The first class is commonly referred to as *dominant function* and the second class, as *dominant preparation*.
   7. Movement within a class does not count as progression. Chord successions within a class often move from diatonic to chromatic or from triad to seventh chord, as in the progressions IV–V/V or ii–ii7.
   8. Some of the more common elisions and retrogressions are vii°–iii, vi–V, V–vi, iii–IV, and IV–I.
   9. The final goal of harmonic progression is always the tonic triad.

III. General comments on chord progression.

   A. In harmonization, a preponderance of normal progression is usually desirable.

   B. In general, more than two successive non-normal progressions should be avoided.

   C. A retrogression (such as V–IV) is often followed by a normal progression back to the first chord (V–IV–V).

   D. Chord change over a bar line is usually desirable.

   E. Successive non-normal progressions (V6–IV6–iii6 and so forth) are usually the result of linear activity, especially sequence.

   F. Generally, the slowest harmonic rhythm appropriate to a given melody will be most effective.

   G. Harmonic rhythm also depends heavily on tempo, character of the melody, and complexity of texture.

9 Figured-Bass Symbols

I. General comments on figured-bass symbols.

    A. Arabic numbers below bass notes (*figured-bass symbols*) indicate intervals formed between the bass and the upper voices.

    B. The figured-bass symbols do not indicate doubling, spacing, or compound intervals.

    C. The numbers 8, 5, and 3 do not usually appear except to cancel a previous symbol under the same bass note.

    D. The numbers 9, 7, 6, 4, and 2 must appear when needed.

II. Specific details.

    A. A bass note with no numbers indicates a root position triad, of which the given note is the root.

    B. A bass note with the numbers 6 or $\frac{6}{3}$ indicates a first-inversion triad, of which the given note is the third.

    C. A bass note with the numbers $\frac{6}{4}$ indicates a second-inversion triad, of which the given note is the fifth. The figures $\frac{5}{3}$ sometimes appear next to cancel the $\frac{6}{4}$, as in the progression $I\frac{6}{4}$–V.

    D. The figures for seventh chords are as follows.
        1. The figure 7 indicates a root position seventh chord.
        2. The figure $\frac{6}{5}$ indicates a first-inversion seventh chord.
        3. The figures $\frac{4}{3}$ or $\frac{6}{4}$ indicate a second-inversion seventh chord.
        4. The figures $\frac{4}{2}$ or 2 indicate a third-inversion seventh chord.

E. An accidental by itself (not immediately next to a number) in the figured bass refers to the third (or tenth or seventeenth) above the bass.

F. Any accidental above the bass must appear in the figured-bass symbols. Alterations to the bass itself cannot appear in the symbols. Any interval above the bass can be raised or lowered by the appropriate accidental symbol.

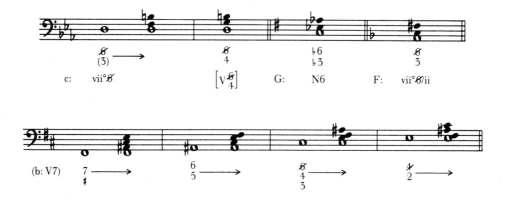

10 Procedure for Harmonizing a Figured Bass

$$6 \qquad 6 \qquad\qquad\qquad \begin{smallmatrix}4\\3\end{smallmatrix} \quad 6 \quad \begin{smallmatrix}6\\5\end{smallmatrix} \quad \begin{smallmatrix}6\\4\end{smallmatrix} \quad 7$$

I. Supply roman numerals.

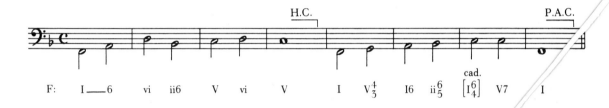

F:　I——6　vi　ii6　V　vi　V　I　V$\frac{4}{3}$　I6　ii$\frac{6}{5}$　[I$\frac{6}{4}$] (cad.)　V7　I

II. Construct the soprano melody. Be attentive to phrasing, cadences, melodic curve, and the contrapuntal relationship with the bass.

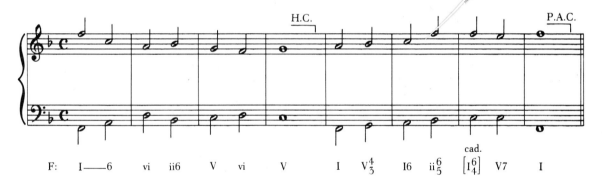

F:　I——6　vi　ii6　V　vi　V　I　V$\frac{4}{3}$　I6　ii$\frac{6}{5}$　[I$\frac{6}{4}$] (cad.)　V7　I

III. Fill in the inner voices. Keep the spacing as consistent as possible and the individual lines as interesting as possible.

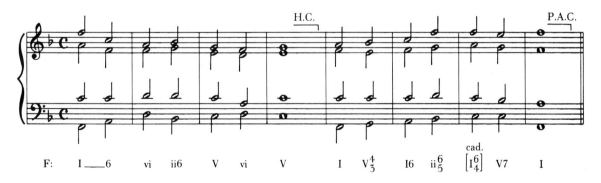

F:　I——6　vi　ii6　V　vi　V　I　V$\frac{4}{3}$　I6　ii$\frac{6}{5}$　[I$\frac{6}{4}$] (cad.)　V7　I

IV. Add embellishments (nonharmonic tones) as appropriate to increase musical interest and provide rhythmic continuity.

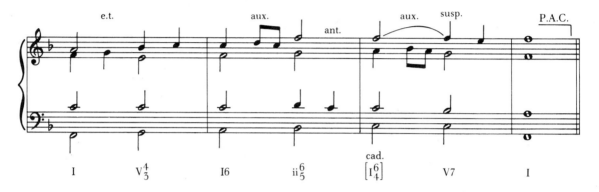

V. Rework the material in IV, employing a motivically consistent instrumental figuration. Keep the same structural elements developed in steps I through IV. This instrumental version is for woodwind quintet:

11 Procedure for Harmonizing a Melody

I. Determine the key, cadences, and phrasing. Supply roman numerals for the cadence. Where more than one chord would work well, supply both choices.

II. Supply roman numerals (*not* inversions at this point) throughout. Work for a fairly consistent harmonic rhythm. In general, the slowest harmonic rhythm (that is, speed and pattern of chord change) appropriate to the harmonic implications of the melody and the tempo will work best. Where more than one chord would work well, supply both choices. Determine which notes, if any, in the melody are to be treated as nonharmonic.

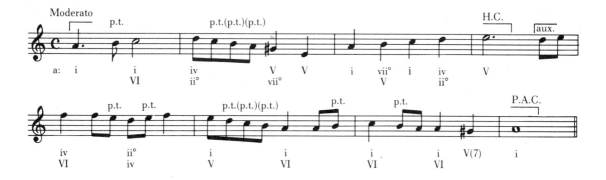

III. Construct the bass line. Be attentive to phrasing, cadences, good linear interest, and the contrapuntal relationship with the soprano melody. It is at this stage that the precise chord choices (where there is more than one possibility) and inversion choices are made.

Observe here the following:

A. The bass note changes over the bar line.

B. The harmonic rhythm reinforces the meter.

C. The harmonic rhythm is consistent in the first two measures of each phrase, quickens in the measure that precedes the cadence, and comes to rest at the cadence point.

IV. Fill in the inner voices. Keep the spacing as consistent as possible and the individual lines as interesting as possible.

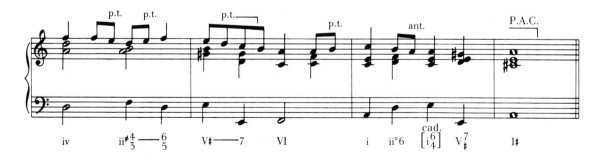

V. Add embellishments (nonharmonic tones) to the lower three voices as appropriate to increase musical interest and rhythmic continuity. Note the consistent eighth note motion, continuing across the bar lines and into the cadences.

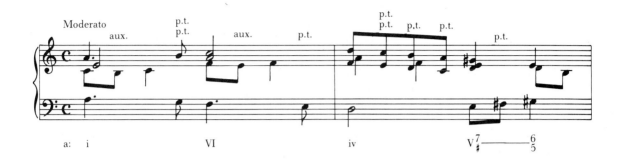

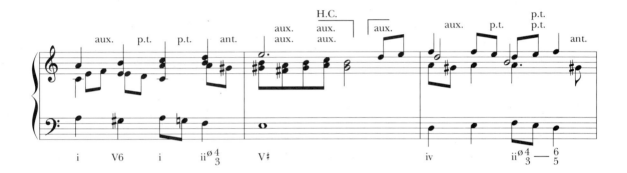

VI. Rework the material in V, employing a motivically consistent instrumental figuration. Keep the same structural elements developed in steps I through V. This instrumental version is for piano:

12 Models for Expansion and Elaboration

The following procedure may be used for expansion and elaboration with the chord-phrase formats and figured or unfigured basses:

D major: $\frac{4}{4}$ I ii6 | $\left[\text{I}^6_4 \right]$ cad. V7 | I ‖

I. Provide outer voices.

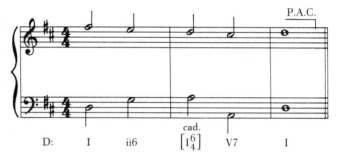

II. Complete the basic part-writing.

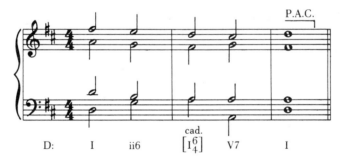

III. Further expand the basic part-writing.

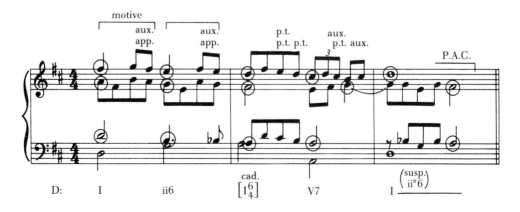

IV. Finally, use more textural expansion, a new soprano line, a more linear bass line, and fuller harmony. Edit fully.

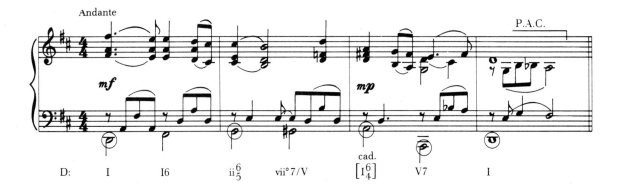

13 Cadence and Phrase Structure

I. The *cadence* is one important means of formal articulation; it is a point of arrival or rest in the musical flow. Cadences may be *medial* (requiring continuation) or *final*.

   A. *Authentic cadence* (medial or final).

      1. A *perfect authentic cadence* (P.A.C.) is usually final. Its conditions follow: V (or V7)–I, both chords are in root position, and the tonic note is in the upper voice in the I chord.

      2. An *imperfect authentic cadence* (I.A.C.) is usually medial. Its conditions follow: V (V7)–I, either or both are in inversion; V (V7)–I, with a note other than the tonic note in the upper voice with the I chord; or vii° (vii°7)–I.

      3. A *half cadence* (H.C. or *semicadence*) is medial only and includes any cadence ending on a dominant function chord, such as IV–V, ii–V, I–V, vi–V, or V/V–V (others are possible).

      4. A *deceptive cadence* (D.C.), such as V–vi, V–IV6, or V–V7/V (others are possible), substitutes for, and is usually closely followed by, an expected authentic cadence.

      5. A *plagal cadence* (P.C.) is usually final, following an authentic cadence: IV–I, ii–I, or ii7–I.

      6. A *phrygian cadence* is the progression iv6–V♯ in a minor key, when used as a terminal progression.

II. Phrase structure and period form.

   A. A *phrase* is a musical thought ending with a partial or complete point of rest.

   B. A *period* is two phrases, usually of the same length, forming a complete musical thought. The constituent phrases normally form a question-answer (antecedent-consequent) relationship such that phrase 2 completes and complements phrase 1. The first cadence will usually be weaker than the second. The structure of the period is often as follows:

	H.C. or I.A.C.		I.A.C. or P.A.C.
Phrase 1	⌐	Phrase 2	⌐

Periods are classified by a comparison of the beginnings of the two phrases, which will either be the same *(parallel period)*, distinctly different *(contrasting period)*, sequentially related *(sequential period)*, or inversionally related *(inverted period)*. A double period, consisting of two periods, is graphed here:

	I.A.C. or H.C.	H.C. or I.A.C.		H.C.	P.A.C.
Period 1	⌐	⌐	Period 2	⌐	⌐

Either phrase 1 or phrase 2 may be repeated, or a cadential expansion may extend phrase 2. Periods often modulate to closely related key areas.

   C. A *phrase-group (phrase chain)* is a series of two or more related phrases that do not form a clear periodic structure.

14 Typical Phrase Variants

Composers generally avoid excessive regularity or squareness of phrase. Some typical variants follow.

I. *Regular phrase structure can be varied through a process of inner expansion by the following means:*

A. Repetition of a figure.

Capriccio   Haydn

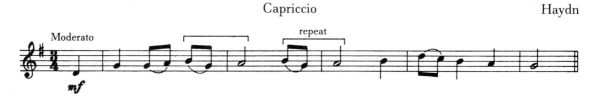

B. Sequential expansion of a figure.

1.

String Quartet, op. 17, no. 5   Haydn

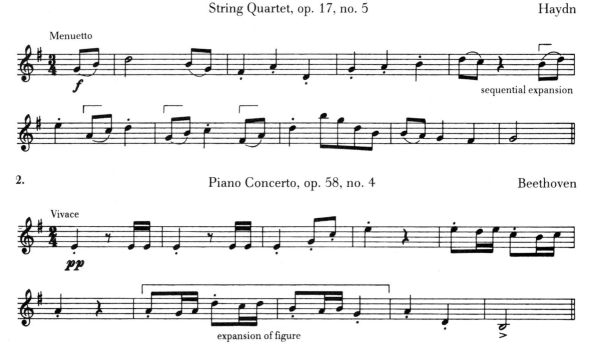

2.

Piano Concerto, op. 58, no. 4   Beethoven

C. Interpolation of an "extra" measure or two.

The Magic Flute, act 2, no. 18   Mozart

II. Formal elision, whereby the last beat of a phrase becomes the first beat of the following phrase, is a common device.

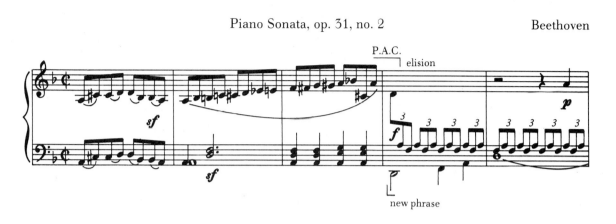

Piano Sonata, op. 31, no. 2 — Beethoven

III. A phrase or period may be expanded at the end by several means.

    A. Cadential extension, often by repeating the cadential figure following a D.C. or I.A.C.

O Cessate di Piagarmi — A. Scarlatti

    B. Expansion (lengthening) of the cadential figure.

Piano Sonata, op. 2, no. 1 — Beethoven

15 The Motive

I. A *motive* (M) may be defined as a relatively short musical idea that functions as a cell or basic unit from which phrases and larger structural units are constructed. The motive is characterized by its rhythmic shape, its intervals, and its harmonic implication. A motive may display only one of these characteristics (for example, rhythm alone), or it may display a combination of characteristics. The motive becomes an important unifying device either by its consistent use throughout a phrase, its use in subsequent phrases, or its use throughout an extended composition. During the course of a piece the motive may undergo considerable alteration or transformation, most frequently during transitional or developmental sections.

II. Common treatments of a motive.

    A. Repetition or recurrence.
       1. The motive may be repeated within a phrase.

Piano Sonata, op. 14, no. 2   Beethoven

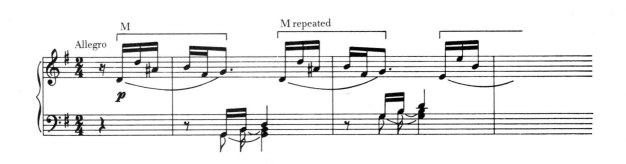

       2. The motive may appear at the beginnings of parallel phrases, transposed or untransposed.

Viola, op. 123   Schubert

3. The motive may appear in accompanying voices.

"An die Musik," op. 88, no. 4   Schubert

B. Change of interval.

1. Interval changes will occur when the motive is restated at different pitch levels with the same underlying harmony.

Piano Sonata in G Minor, no. 4   Haydn

Piano Sonata, K. 547a   Mozart

2. Interval changes will occur when the motive is transposed or altered to accommodate a change in the underlying harmony.

Piano Sonata in D Major, no. 37   Haydn

Waltz, op. 9a, no. 13   Schubert

3. Interval changes will occur when the motive is used sequentially.

The Temple of Glory   Rameau

4. A change of interval often results in a sense of motive expansion.

Piano Trio, op. 1, no. 3   Beethoven

intervals expanded

C. Change of rhythm.

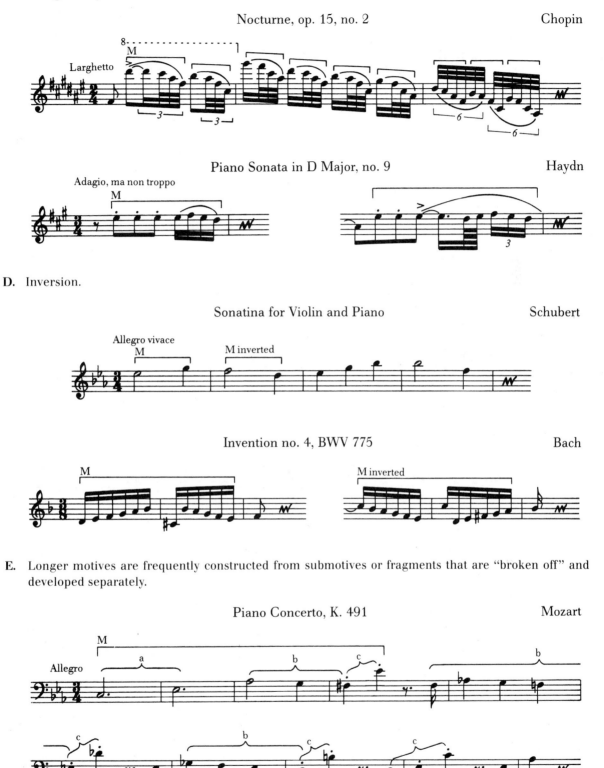

D. Inversion.

E. Longer motives are frequently constructed from submotives or fragments that are "broken off" and developed separately.

Piano Sonata, op. 2, no. 1   Beethoven

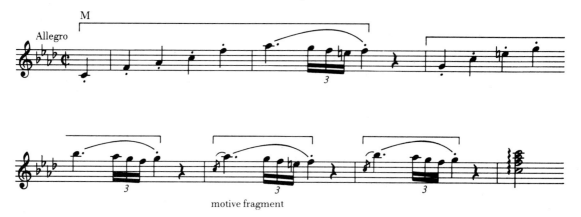

motive fragment

F. Addition of notes; transformation.

Wiegenlied, op. 49, no. 4   Brahms

Note in the following example (Rondo, K. 494) how Mozart progressively ornaments the motive, ulti-
mately using the transformed motive in an imitative passage.

1.

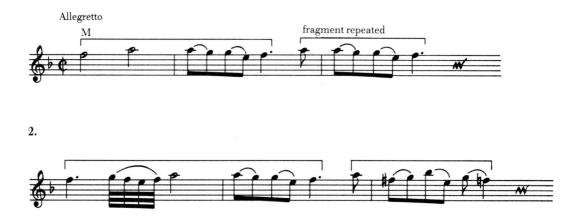

2.

3.

4.

16 The Sequence

I. A *sequence* is the repetition of a musical motive or pattern on successively higher or lower pitch levels. A sequence may occur in only one voice, but most frequently it involves all voices or elements of the texture. Certain chord progressions are typically elaborated sequentially; in other instances the sequential lines themselves give rise to linear progressions (those having nonfunctional root motion).

II. Common sequential progressions.

    A. Sequences typically occur with a series of chords related by root motion of a descending fifth. When all the diatonic triads or seventh chords occur in this context, the IV and vii° will not have their more usual functions.

        1. Diatonic triads.

Piano Sonata, K. 545 — Mozart

In the minor mode, note that the VII is a major triad built on the unaltered seventh scale-degree.

Sonata in A Minor for Recorder and Continuo, no. 4 of Fifteen Solos, op. 1 — Handel

III6　　　　　　VI　　　　　　ii°6　　　　V♯　　V♯⁷　　vii°7

2. Diatonic seventh chords.

Organ Concerto in D Minor　　　　　　Vivaldi-Bach

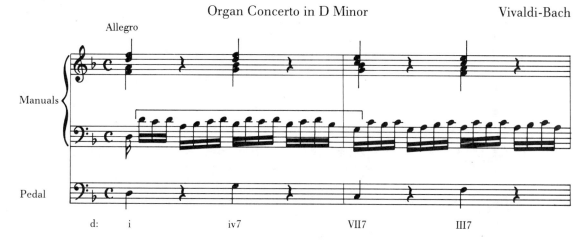

d:　i　　　　　iv7　　　　　VII7　　　　　III7

VI7　　　ii♯7　　　　v7　　　　i7　　　　VI6

Piano Sonatina, op. 88, no. 3　　　　　　Kuhlau

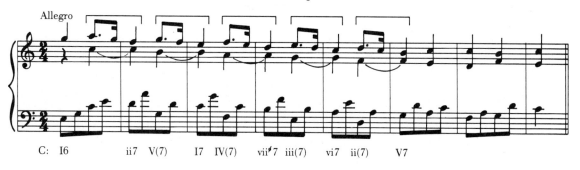

C:　I6　　　ii7　V(7)　　I7　IV(7)　vii♯7　iii(7)　vi7　ii(7)　V7

3. Diatonic chords and secondary dominants in combination.
   a. Nonmodulating.

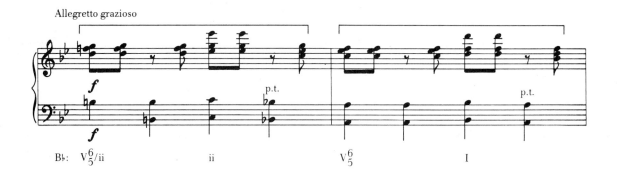

Bb: V$^6_5$/ii   ii   V$^6_5$ I

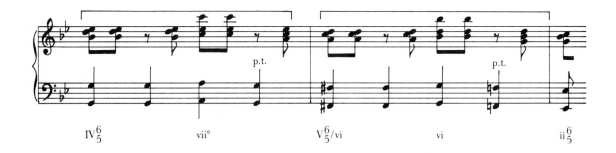

IV$^6_5$ vii°   V$^6_5$/vi   vi   ii$^6_5$

   b. Modulating.

"Danza, danza, fanciulla gentile"

Durante

Dan - za, __ dan - za, fan - ciul - la, __ al __ mi - o can - tar; dan - za, __

Dance, O __ dance, maid - en gay, to __ the __ song that I sing; dance, __ O __

bb: i   V$^6_5$/VII

B. Sequences can involve linear progressions.

    1. By thirds.

Intermezzo, op. 119, no. 3   Brahms

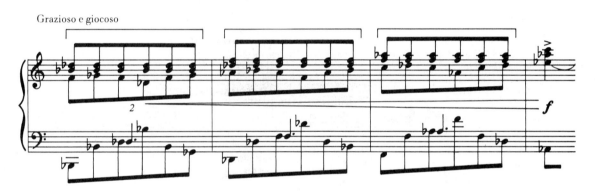

    2. By seconds.

"Il nocchier nella Tempesta" from *Salustia*, act 2, scene 9   Pergolesi

Textures

I. *Monophonic texture* consists of a single line, or lines doubled at the unison or octave, occurring for only one or two beats or for several measures:

II. *Chordal texture* consists predominantly of *block chords,* or all voices moving in the same rhythm.

    A.   Simple four-voice texture.

    B.   Simple three-voice texture may be considered a reduction of four-voice texture. Chords are either triads with no doublings or triads with one tone omitted and conventional doubling (for example, doubled root). Four-voice texture is often implied by skips in one or more of the lines.

C. *Multiple doublings* are one or more lines doubled at the octave, or expansion to five or more voices.*

D. Keyboard textures are often free, with the texture varying frequently, generally by "filling out" certain chords or as a result of adding or dropping lines.

III. In a solo with accompaniment, the solo element may be a single line, may be duplicated with parallel intervals, or may be harmonized in close spacing. Note that normal voice-leading procedures are followed in the accompanying voices, or the voices are implied by a broken chord pattern.

---

*Much passage work in keyboard music can be related to an elaboration of multiple doublings.

A. Simple chords.

B. Dance style (stride piano or "boom-chuck" patterns).

C. Broken chord patterns.

IV. *Polyphonic texture* consists of two or more equal and independent lines. Often the lowest line functions specifically as a bass line; at other times it is an equal melodic line; often it combines both aspects. Polyphonic textures often occur in alternation with chordal textures, thus providing an additional element of contrast or variety. Occasionally, one or more voices will be duplicated (harmonized) with parallel intervals.

18 An Introduction to Tonal Melody

I. Tonal melody uses three types of melodic motion: repetition of pitches, arpeggiation of triads, and stepwise (scalar) motion.

Piano Sonata in D Major, no. 9 — Haydn

Adagio, ma non troppo
repetition   aux. p.t.

Die Schöne Müllerin, op. 25, no. 2 — Schubert

Mässig   arpeggiation

Piano Trio, op. 97 — Beethoven

Scherzo   scalar motion

Piano Sonatina IV in F Major — Haydn

Scherzo   combination

II. The formal structure of melody is related to the underlying harmonic framework. Cadences are an interaction of harmonic and melodic activity; harmonic goals have their counterpart in melodic goals. A melodic half cadence commonly uses either the supertonic or leading tone; a perfect authentic cadence, the tonic, and so forth.

III. The range of many melodies falls within the area bounded by the tonic and its octave or the dominant and its octave. Notes outside this area are used sparingly, with the highest and lowest notes occurring only once or twice.* The rise and fall of the line within this limit is called the *melodic curve* or *waveline*. Occasionally a

---

*Important exceptions to this are found in piano and instrumental literature, especially that of a soloistic or virtuosic nature.

melody will exhibit a very narrow range, or static waveline, but in this case other elements (for example, contrapuntal activity or highly rhythmic character) compensate for the lack of curve.

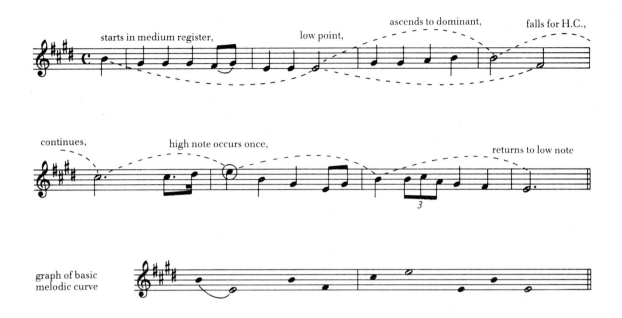

IV. Rhythmic motion through the phrase is achieved by using quicker notes on weak beats to carry the music across the bar line. Agogic accents (accents by duration) generally coincide with metric accents; syncopation and the use of longer notes on weak beats create variety or special effects.* Most melodies use only one or two basic rhythmic patterns or motives with variations coming toward the cadence points, where the motion is often increased. If one phrase begins with an upbeat, so will subsequent phrases, and the upbeat figure will probably recur throughout the phrase.

Piano Trio, op. 1, no. 3   Beethoven

---

*Certain dances have particular patterns with a stressed second beat in triple meter, for example, the saraband and mazurka.

V. The style characteristics of the melody are determined by the medium and purpose for which the melody is composed, the texture, and so forth, as well as by the type of expression the composer desires. The one general criterion would seem to be the unity of style. The type of expression desired plays an important role in determining the use of nonharmonic tones.

A. The use of simple weak passing tones and auxiliaries results in a harmonically straightforward, "masculine" line.

Sonatina for Violin and Piano, op. 137, no. 1 — Schubert

B. Melodies using a large number of strong-beat nonharmonic tones have a highly expressive, "feminine" character.

Quartet, K. 428 — Mozart

C. In homophonic music, if the structure of the phrase is clearly delineated by the bass line and accompaniment, the melody may exhibit greater freedom. For example, at a medial cadence the melodic activity often continues through the measure, thus creating a "melodic link" between the two phrases.

String Quartet, op. 3, no. 5 — Haydn

D. In much romantic music and many slow movements of classical works, the melody often takes on a highly ornamental, elaborate, improvisatory character.

Ballade, op. 47, no. 3 — Chopin

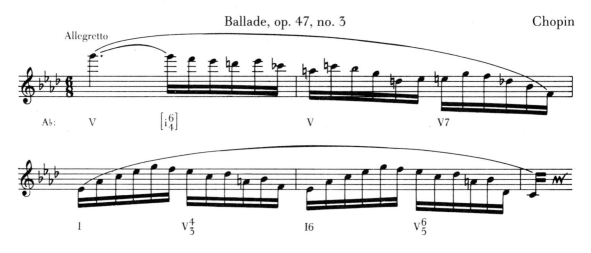

VI. Sample analysis for study.

An den Sonnenschein, op. 36, no. 4   Schumann

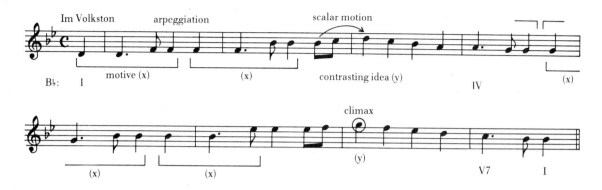

VII. A brief introduction to structural-pitch reduction.

Not all the pitches in a given melody or bass line are equally important. The graphic reduction of a line to its main pitches helps reveal the directional nature of the line, as well as the ways in which line and tonality interact. Although the identification of structural pitches is to some extent subjective, the notes that tend to sound most important in any given line are those that are accented and/or long. These are often tonic triad members and goal notes.

The following structural-pitch reduction is suggested by, but not directly based on, the work of Austrian theorist Heinrich Schenker (1868–1935). The following symbols are used in this reduction:

   ♩   = principal structural pitch (tonic note)

   𝅗𝅥   = secondary pitch

   ●   = decorative pitch

   ⌣   = melodic motion prolonging or connecting structural pitches; these comprise arpeggiation (A), neighboring motion (N), and passing motion (P)

   ⌢→   = prolongations and octave transfers of structural pitches

Dotted lines in this example show the basic scalar motion:

Symphony no. 104 in D Major, fourth movement   Haydn

One possible reduction follows:

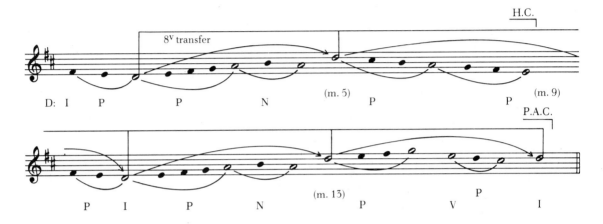

19 An Introduction to Tonal Counterpoint

I. The term *counterpoint* refers to a texture in which the voices exhibit some degree of linear independence. Most music is to some degree contrapuntal.

II. In studying the relationship between two given voices, the following items should be noted.

   A. Note the rhythmic relationship. The voices may proceed in the same note values but are more often rhythmically distinct, frequently in a ratio of 2:1.

Bourrée   Bach

Allegro   Handel

   B. Note relative directions. The voices may run in parallel, similar, oblique, or contrary motion in relation to one another. In most pieces a mixture of all four types prevails, with a slight preference for contrary motion. Parallel perfect consonances are not found, and too many successive parallel imperfect consonances detract from the independence of line.

Bourrée   Bach

Bagatelle, op. 126, no. 5   Beethoven

C. Note vertical (harmonic) intervals. In general, imperfect consonances are preponderant, except at the beginning of a phrase and at cadence points, where perfect unisons, octaves, and fifths are often found. The intervals placed on the beat are usually consonant, except when a nonharmonic tone is clearly heard in one voice.

                                        Allegro   Handel

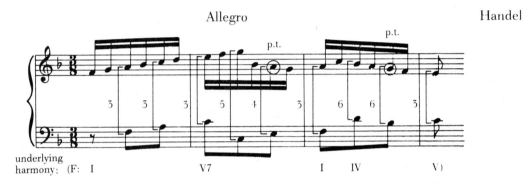

underlying
harmony: (F: I   V7   I   IV   V)

                                Viennese Sonatina   Mozart

        C: ii   V   I   ii6

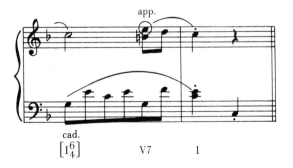

        cad.
        [I⁶₄]   V7   I

---

*Occasionally one or more voices will be coupled at the third or sixth.

The harmonic implications of the most common vertical intervals are as follows: thirds and sixths imply triads, seconds and sevenths imply seventh chords, and tritones imply dominant function.

D. Note *invertible counterpoint*, a technique in which the voices exchange place so that the upper voice becomes the lower.

Sonata, K. 280   Mozart

Sonata, op. 14, no. 1   Beethoven

Sonata, op. 13   Beethoven

E. Note melodic materials.

    1. The voices may have different motivic material.

Tristan und Isolde, Prelude   Wagner

2. The voices may share the same motivic material.

Sonata, K. 280

Mozart

Sonata, Hob. XVI:37

Haydn

Rhapsody, op. 79, no. 1

Brahms

3. *Imitation* is the technique in which the same melodic material is taken up in succession by different voices. Imitative passages are analyzed in terms of the time and pitch intervals between the voices at their entry and the length for which the imitation is carried out. For example, the following Bach invention illustrates imitation at two measures (six beats) at the octave below:

Invention in D Minor   Bach

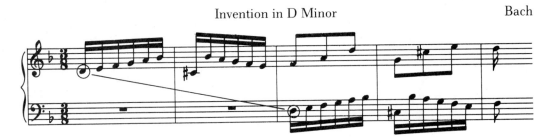

Sonata, op. 2, no. 2   Beethoven

Symphonic Etudes, op. 13   Schumann

Stretto imitation occurs when the imitating voice enters before the first voice has finished its statement, as follows:

Viennese Sonatina   Mozart

Symphonic Etudes, op. 13   Schumann

Intermezzo, op. 118, no. 4   Brahms

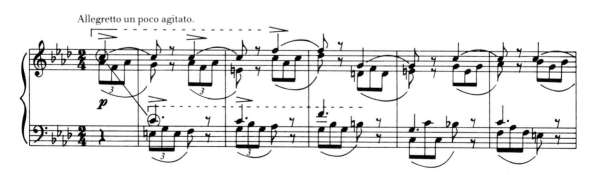

F. Note the harmony. As in the previous examples, the underlying harmony is almost always clear and functional, often with a steady and fairly slow harmonic rhythm.

20 Form

I. *Form* in tonal music is articulated by tonal factors, cadence types and placement, motivic relationships, and sometimes by aspects of texture and color.

II. Typical formal procedures based on counterpoint:

   A. *Cantus firmus* is a procedure in which a pre-existing melody is heard in relatively long tones, around which the other voices move in faster values. Most chorale preludes are of this type.

   B. *Basso ostinato* (ground bass) is a variation technique based on a repeating melodic pattern, usually heard in the lowest voice. The pattern is four, eight, or sixteen measures long, is usually in triple meter, in the minor mode, and moves between the tonic and dominant notes. Passacaglia and chaconne are two common variation forms using ostinato.

   C. A *fugue* is an extended imitative work based on one theme *(subject)*. The first section consists of an *exposition*, with alternating entrances of the subject and the *answer* or *response* (the subject stated at the dominant level). Statements of the subject and answer may be separated by brief linking passages *(codettas)*. There may or may not be a consistent countertheme *(countersubject)* heard with the subject. Following the exposition, the fugue alternates *episodes* (developmental sections, usually sequential and modulatory, based on motivic material from the subject) and *middle entries* of the subject and/or answer in a variety of keys. The subject usually returns in the tonic key near the end. A *double fugue* has two subjects, which are exposed either together at the beginning or in two separate expositions and combined later.

   D. An *invention* is a relatively short imitative piece based on a single melodic idea. As with the fugue, imitative statements of the principal motive alternate with episodic passages based on the motive.

III. *Binary form.*

   A. In *simple binary form*, A B or ‖:A:‖:B:‖, the two sections may be roughly equal in length or the second section may be longer. The first section may modulate to a closely related key, such as the dominant or relative, and therefore is open ended, and the second remodulates to the tonic.

Minuet from Suite no. 1   Purcell

B. In *rounded binary form*, A B A′ or ‖: A :‖: B A′ :‖, the first A section often modulates to the dominant or relative, the B section remodulates and typically ends with a half cadence. They are therefore open ended, and the final A section is complete (closed ended). The B section typically develops material from the A section and either prolongs the V or ends with a half cadence.

Sonata   Haydn

C. *Bar form* is ‖: A :‖ B. The B section is often as long as, or longer than, the repeated A section.

"Nun danket alle Gott"

Johann Crüger

IV. In most *three-part (ternary) forms* the sections are roughly equal in length and independent (closed ended and self-contained). The B section is usually in a closely related key.

Schumann

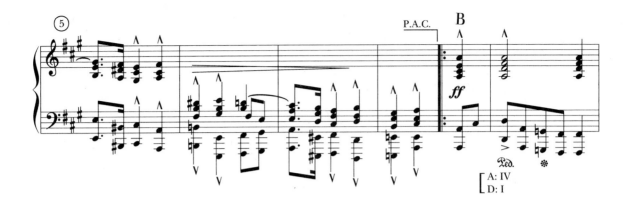

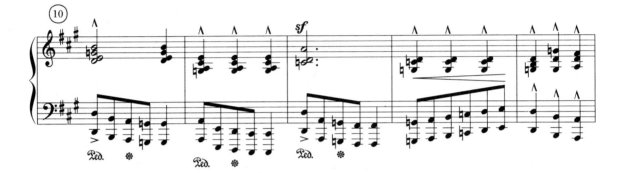

V. In *compound ternary form*, each of the three sections usually consists of a *rounded binary form*. In the following example, the "Da Capo" instruction provides the final $\boxed{A}$ section.

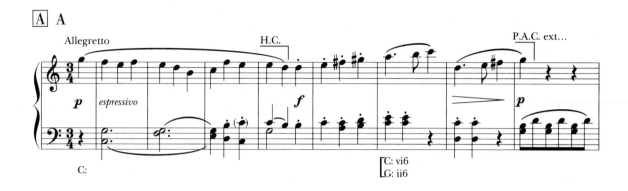

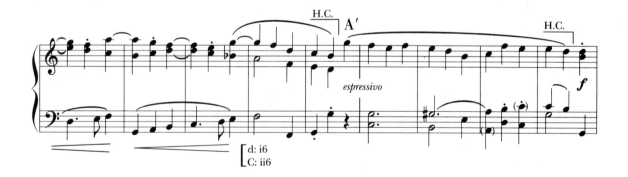

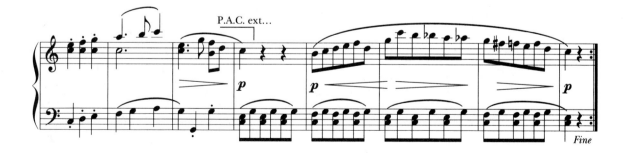

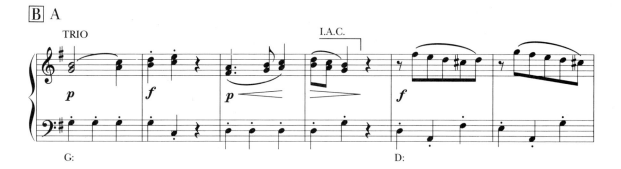

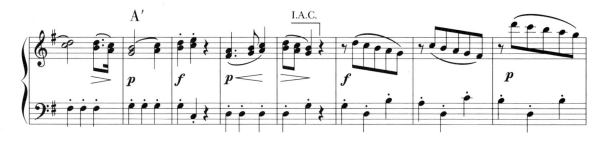

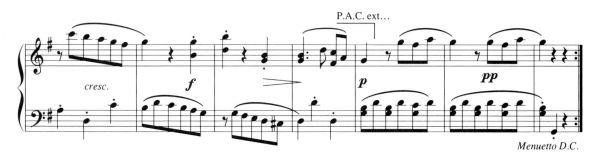

VI. *Sonata form* consists of three large sections: *exposition, development,* and *recapitulation.* The *exposition* consists of the following parts: the *first theme* (A) in the tonic key; the *transition*, which is modulatory; and the *second theme* (B), usually in the dominant key (if the tonic is major) or the relative key (if the tonic is minor). The *second theme* may be followed by an additional theme, or *closing theme*, also in the new key. The *exposition* may be concluded with a *codetta*, which is primarily cadential. The development section develops the material of the exposition, and possibly new material as well. Typically, the development section passes through several keys. At the end of the development there is often a *retransition*; this section re-establishes the tonic key and prepares for the recapitulation, which normally contains the material of the exposition, although with some modifications. The recapitulation normally remains in the tonic key. An *introduction* may occur at the beginning of the form, and a *coda* may occur at the end.

In the following diagram, optional elements of sonata form are presented in parentheses:

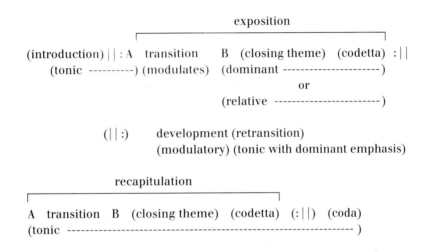

VII. The distinguishing characteristic of *rondo form* is the alternation of an initial section, A, with contrasting sections. The A sections usually occur in the tonic key and the alternating sections, in contrasting keys. Rondos are typically in five or seven parts in the following designs:

A B A C A
A B A B A
A B A C A B A
A B A C A D A

VIII. *Sonata-rondo form* is a seven-part rondo in which the fourth part, C, is developmental. The key plan closely resembles that of sonata form:

A	B	A	C	A	B	A
(tonic)	(dominant	(tonic)	(developmental)	(tonic ----------------------)		
	or		(modulatory)			
	relative)					

21 Checklist for Analysis

All music should be analyzed as fully as possible within the limits of the student's knowledge at any stage of learning. Not only the individual elements, but also their interaction, should be studied. Following is a checklist of elements that should be included in an analysis.

I. Harmonic language.

   A. All keys and chords, with roman numerals and figured-bass symbols, or appropriate contemporary nomenclature. How are the key and mode established?

   B. All modulations, indicating type and placement.

   C. All cadences, indicating type and placement.

   D. All nonharmonic tones, by type.

   E. Functional and nonfunctional use of chromaticism.

   F. Use of nonfunctional (linear or coloristic) chords.

II. Large and small formal units.

   A. Phrases and periods, if any; phrase-groups; extensions and elisions.

   B. Overall form, including large letters for main sections and formal label, if appropriate. Note balance and proportion of sections.

   C. Use of repetition, altered repetition, departure, return, altered return, development, and contrast. Note the use of developmental devices.

   D. Elements of unity versus elements of variety.

   E. Stable versus unstable areas (tension versus relaxation).

III. Melodic organization.

   A. Motivic structure, both melodic and rhythmic.

   B. Melodic structure, including departure note and goal note, contour, climax, main structural pitches, range, and tessitura.

   C. Special aspects, such as contrapuntal devices and sequence.

IV. Rhythmic organization.

   A. Surface rhythm, meter, and harmonic rhythm.

   B. Special devices of rhythmic development.

   C. How the meter is emphasized or obscured.

   D. Tempo.

V. Sound.

A. Use of the medium: idiomatic devices, range and tessitura, and timbre (color).

B. Texture.

C. Dynamics.

VI. Text-setting, where appropriate.

A. Relations between form and/or mood of text and music.

B. Rhythmic and/or metric relationships.

Sample Analysis

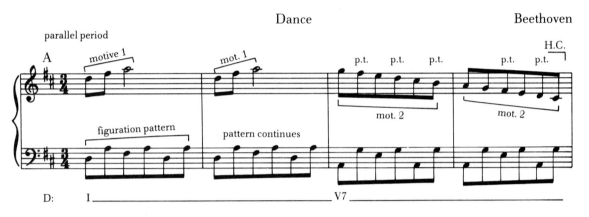

Dance — Beethoven

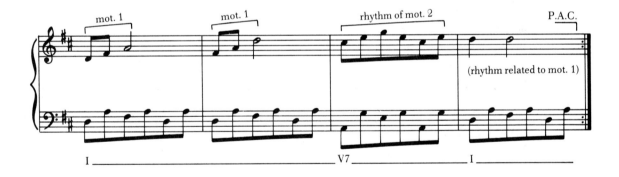

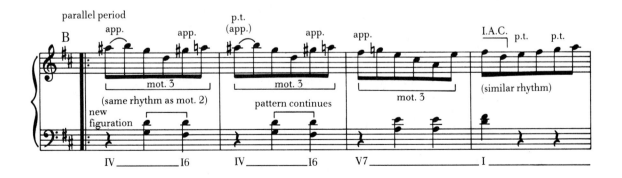

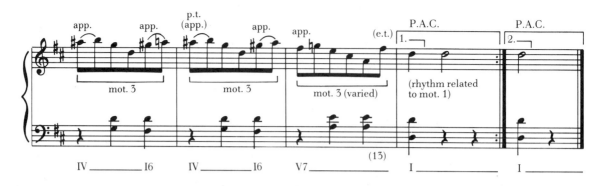

Observations

1. The form is simple binary: ‖: A :‖ : B :‖.
2. Each section is a parallel period consisting of two four-measure phrases.
3. There is new motivic material and a new figuration in the B section.
4. Harmonic rhythm.
    a. A section: slow.

    𝅗𝅥. | 𝅗𝅥. for the first six measures.

    𝅗𝅥. for the last two measures.

    b. B section: faster, slowing at cadence.

    𝅗𝅥 𝅘𝅥 | 𝅗𝅥 𝅘𝅥 | 𝅗𝅥. | 𝅗𝅥. (each phrase)

5. The background rhythm consists of eighth note motion throughout, passing from the accompanimental figuration in the A section to the melodic material in the B section and coming to rest in the final measure.

VII. The following aspects of any tonal contrapuntal work should be carefully observed and analyzed.

A. Individual lines.
    1. Main motives (melodic and rhythmic).
    2. Melodic intervals (types used and their placement in the phrase).
    3. Cadence idioms.
    4. Sequences (length, number of repetitions, and transposition).
    5. Compound line, if any.
    6. Climax placement.
    7. Main structural pitches.

B. Relationships between lines.
    1. Directional relationships (contrary, parallel, similar, or oblique).
    2. Rhythmic relationships.
    3. Motivic relationships (imitation, or bass line, with predominant melody).
    4. Intervallic relationships (on both strong and weak beats, as well as at cadence points; analyze all dissonances carefully).
    5. Harmonic relationships (keys and harmonic implications, in roman numerals).

Gavotte I from English Suite no. 3

J. S. Bach

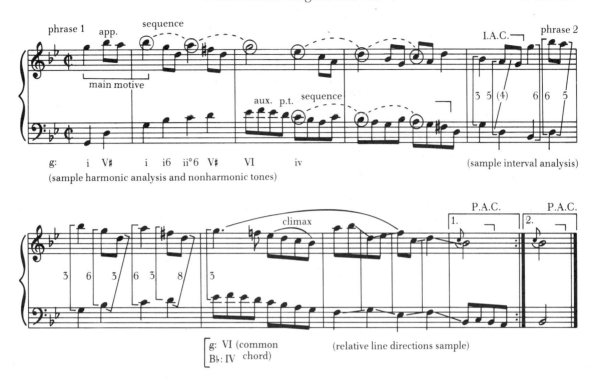

(sample harmonic analysis and nonharmonic tones)

(sample interval analysis)

(relative line directions sample)

Observations

1. The form is the first half of a binary suite movement, modulating to the relative key by common chord (measure 6). Measures 1 through 8 form a parallel period.
2. Main motive.

3. Reduction to principal structural pitches (for an explanation of symbols, see Part V, Unit 18).

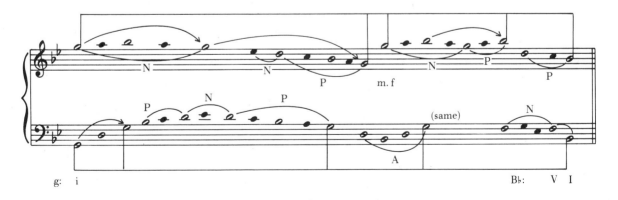

4. Other observations.
    a. The bass line is largely independent and nonimitative.
    b. Melodically, seconds and thirds predominate.
    c. There is a mixture of types of directional relationships, with no single type predominating.
    d. Rhythmically the voices are about equally active, with the upper voice only slightly dominant.
    e. Imperfect consonances predominate between voices except at cadence points, where there are tonic notes.
    f. Nonharmonic tones are mainly passing tones and neighbors.
    g. Notice the typical cadential figure in the bass in measures 7 and 8.
    h. The upper voice forms a compound line in measures 1, 2, 3, 5, and 7.

VIII. The following are additional questions for the analysis of twentieth-century music.
    A. Tonal centers, if any.
        1. How are they established?
        2. Do they change?

    B. Scalar materials.
        1. What type or types are employed?
        2. Do they change, or are they inflected?

    C. Harmonic vocabulary.
        1. What type of chord structures are used?
        2. Is chord succession systematic? If so, how?

    D. Special metric and rhythmic characteristics.

22 Composition Checklist

This list should be used for reference when doing the free creative projects suggested in this book. Some of the following considerations may not apply in the early stages or in Part IV.

I. Form.

    A. Sections (tonal, cadential, or thematic) are clearly articulated.

    B. Phrases are clear and generally regular.

    C. The climax is clear and well placed.

    D. Contrast, repetition, and return are used where appropriate.

    E. All sections are proportionally balanced.

II. Harmony.

    A. Types of cadences are clear, well placed, and prepared.

    B. Functional progressions predominate.

    C. The harmonic rhythm generally is steady and regular.

    D. Altered chords are well placed in the phrase and not overused.

    E. Nonharmonic tone use is normal (motivic or sequential).

III. Line.

    A. There is a sense of contour (departure, curve, and arrival).

    B. There is a clear tonal organization.

    C. There is a linear and directional bass line.

    D. The outer-voice contrapuntal framework is effective.

    E. The motivic control (melodic and rhythmic) is tight.

    F. There is thematic clarity and consistency.

IV. Rhythm.

    A. There is metrical clarity and consistency.

    B. The rhythm is steady and regular, with a clear feeling of pattern.

    C. Rhythmic motion continues over weak cadence points.

V. Other matters.

    A. Accompaniment patterns are appropriate and consistent.

    B. There is overall textural consistency.

C. There is thematic balance between players, where appropriate.

D. Instrumental and vocal writing is idiomatic.

E. The editing of score and parts is careful and complete.

F. Notation is clear and complete.

G. There is normal word and syllable stress in text-setting.

H. Careful attention is paid to transpositions.

I. There is appropriate use of dynamics and tempo gradations.

23 Instrumental Ranges and Transpositions

The registers indicated here are recommended for classroom use.

Woodwinds	Written Range	Actual Sound

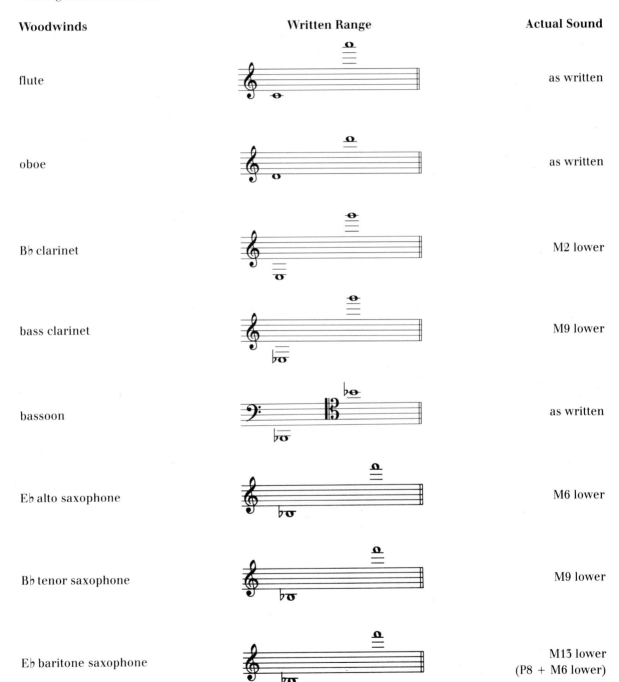

flute		as written
oboe		as written
Bb clarinet		M2 lower
bass clarinet		M9 lower
bassoon		as written
Eb alto saxophone		M6 lower
Bb tenor saxophone		M9 lower
Eb baritone saxophone		M13 lower (P8 + M6 lower)

Brass	Written Range	Actual Sound
French horn in F		P5 lower
B♭ trumpet		M2 lower (C trumpet = as written)
trombone euphonium		as written
tuba		as written

Strings	Written Range	Actual Sound
violin		as written
viola		as written
cello		as written
double bass		P8 lower

Bibliography

Important General Works

Bent, Ian, with William Drabkin. *Analysis.* New York: Norton, 1987.

Berry, Wallace. *Form in Music.* Englewood Cliffs, N.J.: Prentice-Hall, 1966.

Dunsby, Jonathan, and Arnold Whittall. *Music Analysis in Theory and Practice.* New Haven: Yale University Press, 1988.

Goldman, Richard Franko. *Harmony in Western Music.* New York: Norton, 1965.

Green, Douglass. *Form in Tonal Music.* 2nd ed. New York: Holt, Rinehart and Winston, 1979.

Karkoschka, Erhard. *Notation in New Music: a critical guide to interpretation and realisation.* Translated by Ruth Koenig. New York: Praeger, 1972.

Kohs, Ellis B. *Musical Form: Studies in Analysis and Synthesis.* Boston: Houghton Mifflin, 1976.

LaRue, Jan. *Guidelines for Style Analysis.* New York: Norton, 1971.

Read, Gardner. *Music Notation: a manual of modern practice.* 2nd ed. New York: Taplinger, 1979.

Salzer, Felix. *Structural Hearing.* New York: Dover, 1952.

Schenker, Heinrich. *Five Graphic Musical Analyses.* New York: Dover, 1969.

_____. *Harmony.* Ed. Jonas Oswald. Trans. Elizabeth Burgese. Chicago: University of Chicago Press, 1980.

Schoenberg, Arnold. *Structural Functions of Harmony.* Ed. Leonard Stein. Rev. ed. New York: Norton, 1969.

Stone, Kurt. *Music Notation in the Twentieth Century.* New York: Norton, 1980.

Toch, Ernst. *Shaping Forces in Music.* Hackensack, N.J.: Criterion Music, 1948.

Counterpoint

Benjamin, Thomas. *Counterpoint in the Style of J. S. Bach.* New York: Schirmer Books, 1986.

Kennan, Kent. *Counterpoint.* 3rd ed. Englewood Cliffs, N.J.: Prentice-Hall, 1987.

Mason, Neale B. *Essentials of Eighteenth-Century Counterpoint.* Dubuque: William C. Brown, 1968.

Piston, Walter. *Counterpoint.* New York: Norton, 1947.

Rudiments Workbooks

Clough, John. *Scales, Intervals, Keys, and Triads.* Rev. ed. New York: Norton, 1983.

Dallin, Leon. *Foundations in Music Theory.* 2nd ed. Belmont, Calif.: Wadsworth, 1967.

Harder, Paul. *Basic Materials in Music Theory.* 2nd ed. Boston: Allyn and Bacon, 1981.

Nelson, Robert, and Carl Christensen. *Foundations of Music: a computer-assisted introduction.* Belmont: Wadsworth Publishing Company, 1987.

Reed, H. Owen. *A Workbook in the Fundamentals of Music.* New York: Mills Music, 1946.

Twentieth-Century Techniques

Brindle, Reginald Smith. *Serial Composition.* London: Oxford University Press, 1966.

Cope, David. *New Directions in Music.* 5th ed. Dubuque: William C. Brown, 1988.

_____. *New Music Composition.* 4th ed. New York: Schirmer Books, 1983.

Dallin, Leon. *Techniques of Twentieth Century Composition.* 3rd ed. Dubuque: William C. Brown, 1974.

Delone, Richard, et al., eds. *Aspects of Twentieth-Century Music.* Englewood Cliffs, N.J.: Prentice-Hall, 1974.

Forte, Allen. *The Structure of Atonal Music.* New Haven: Yale University Press, 1977.

Hanson, Howard. *Harmonic Materials of Modern Music.* New York: Appleton-Century-Crofts, 1960.

Hindemith, Paul. *The Craft of Musical Composition.* New York: Eur-Am Music, 1942 (Book I) and 1941 (Book II).

Lester, Joel. *Analytic Approaches to Twentieth-Century Music.* New York: Norton, 1989.

Nyman, Michael. *Experimental Music.* New York: Schirmer Books, 1975.

Perle, George. *Serial Composition and Atonality.* 5th ed. Berkeley: University of California Press, 1981.

Persichetti, Vincent. *Twentieth Century Harmony.* New York: Norton, 1961.

Reti, Rudolph. *Tonality in Modern Music.* New York: Macmillan, 1962.

Ulehla, Ludmilla. *Contemporary Harmony.* New York: Free Press, 1966.

Electronic Music

Adams, Robert T. *Electronic Music Composition.* Dubuque: William C. Brown, 1986.

Dodge, Charles, and Thomas A. Jarse. *Computer Music.* New York: Schirmer Books, 1985.

Hofstetter, Fred T. *Computer Literacy for Musicians.* Englewood Cliffs, N.J.: Prentice-Hall, 1988.

Moore, Richard. *Elements of Computer Music.* Englewood Cliffs, N.J.: Prentice-Hall, 1990.

Schwartz, Elliott. *Electronic Music.* New York: Praeger, 1985.

Strange, Allen. *Electronic Music.* 2nd ed. Dubuque: William C. Brown, 1982.

Winsor, Phil. *Computer Assisted Music Composition.* Princeton, N.J.: Petrocelli Books, 1990.

Musical Anthologies

Benjamin, Thomas, Michael Horvit, and Robert Nelson. *Music for Analysis: Examples from the Common-Practice Period and the Twentieth Century.* 3rd ed. Boston: Houghton-Mifflin, 1992.

Berry, Wallace, and Edward Chudacoff. *Eighteenth-Century Imitative Counterpoint.* Englewood Cliffs, N.J.: Prentice-Hall, 1969.

Brandt, William, Arthur Corsa, William Christ, Richard Delone, and Allen Winold. *The Comprehensive Study of Music.* New York: Harper & Row, 1976.

Burkhart, Charles. *Anthology for Musical Analysis.* 4th ed. New York: Holt, Rinehart and Winston, 1986.

Cohen, Albert, and John D. White. *Anthology of Music for Analysis.* New York: Appleton-Century-Crofts, 1965.

Hardy, Gordon, and Arnold Fish. *Music Literature.* New York: Dodd, Mead, 1966.

Murphy, Howard, Robert Melcher, and Willard Warch. *Music for Study.* 2nd ed. Englewood Cliffs, N.J.: Prentice-Hall, 1973.

Walton, Charles. *Music Literature for Analysis and Study.* Belmont, Calif.: Wadsworth, 1973.

Wennerstrom, Mary. *Anthology of Twentieth Century Music.* New York: Appleton-Century-Crofts, 1969.

Orchestration

Adler, Samuel. *The Study of Orchestration.* New York: Norton, 1982.

Jacob, Gordon. *Elements of Orchestration.* New York: October House, 1965.

Kennan, Kent, and Donald Grantham. *The Technique of Orchestration.* 3rd ed. Englewood Cliffs, N.J.: Prentice-Hall, 1983.

Piston, Walter. *Orchestration.* New York: Norton, 1955.

Index

December
1995

That's all for today—
here are the
family words
we've talked about...

ADOPT:	to make a child a member of the family.
AUNT:	the sister of your mother or father.
BROTHER:	a male child of your parents.
COUSIN:	first cousin—the child of your aunt and uncle.
	first cousin once removed—the child of your first cousin.
	second cousin—the child of the first cousin of either of your parents.
FAMILY TREE:	a diagram of family members.
FATHER:	your male parent.
GRANDPARENTS:	grandfather—the father of either parent.
	grandmother—the mother of either parent.
GREAT-AUNT:	a sister of one of your grandparents.
GREAT-UNCLE:	a brother of one of your grandparents.
GREAT-GRANDPARENTS:	great-grandfather—the father of one of your grandparents.
	great-grandmother—the mother of one of your grandparents.
HALF BROTHER:	a male child with the same mother or father as you (not both).
HALF SISTER:	a female child with the same mother or father as you (not both).
HUSBAND:	a male spouse.
MOTHER:	your female parent.
NEPHEW:	the male child of your sister or brother.
NIECE:	the female child of your sister or brother.
PARENT:	a father or mother who gives birth to or raises a child.
SISTER:	a female child of your parents.
SPOUSE:	a marriage partner; a husband or wife.
STEPBROTHER:	the male child of your stepparent.
STEPPARENTS:	stepfather—the husband of your divorced or widowed mother.
	stepmother—the wife of your divorced or widowed father.
STEPSISTER:	the female child of your stepparent.
UNCLE:	the brother of your mother or father.
WIFE:	a female spouse.

You know that a first cousin is the child of your aunt and uncle, right?

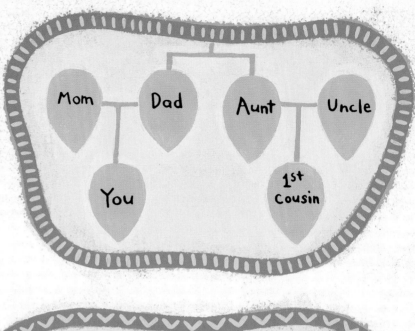

Your second cousin is the child of either <u>parent's</u> first cousin.

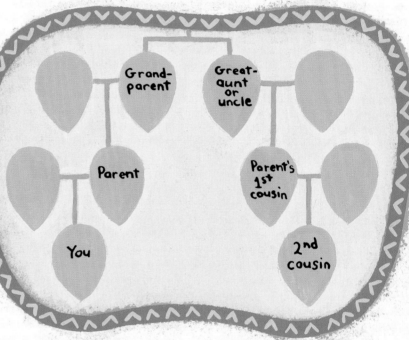

When <u>your</u> first cousin has a child, he or she is your "first cousin once removed."

It's easier just to call them all "cousins."

Thank you all for sharing. It's fun to learn about families. Does anybody have a question?
What is a second cousin?

My mom and my
stepfather had
two kids, so I have
a half brother and
a half sister...

It's pretty crowded at dinnertime!

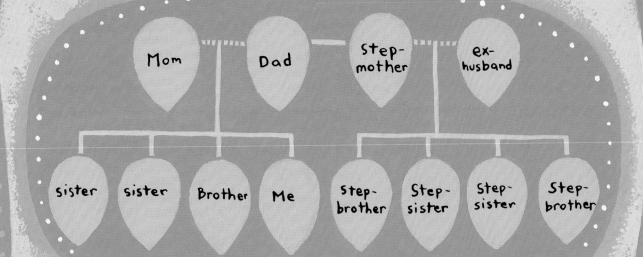

Before my stepmother married my dad, she already had kids — they are my stepbrothers and stepsisters.

My parents got divorced and then Mom got married again. Her husband is my stepfather. Dad's new wife is my stepmother.

My mom and dad adopted me when I was one day old and made me a member of their family.

Thank you for telling us about your family tree, Sandy. Of course, everyone's family is different. Were any of you adopted?

The only one who is still alive is Great-grandma Lou.

She is my mother's mother's mother!

These are my
great-grandparents,
who are my
grandparents'
moms and dads.

Great-uncle Zeke likes to show me his old photographs.

I also have great-aunts and great-uncles, who are my grandparents' brothers and sisters.

When all the cousins come over, our house overflows!

Uncle Aunt Mom Dad Uncle Aunt

Cousin Cousin Cousin Me Cousin Cousin

These are my five first cousins—Tippy, Snowball, Whiskers, Mittens, and Ralph. They are the children of my aunts and uncles.

Aunt Rose and I play dress-up with her old clothes.

I have three aunts and two uncles, who are my parents' brothers and sisters (and their spouses).

Grandma and Grandpa took me to the zoo.

Nanna and Pop-pop took me to the fair.

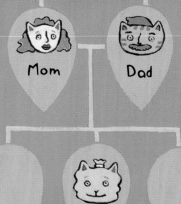

Here are my grandparents.
Grandma and Grandpa are my
mom's parents.
Nanna and Pop-pop
are my dad's
parents.

Sometimes we play together.

Sometimes we fight.

My parents say that I was a perfect baby, usually.

Mom's hobby is gardening.

Dad has an aquarium.

Mom

Dad

Me

This is me, and here are Mom and Dad. Their names are Fluffy Lou and Edward T. Fuzz.

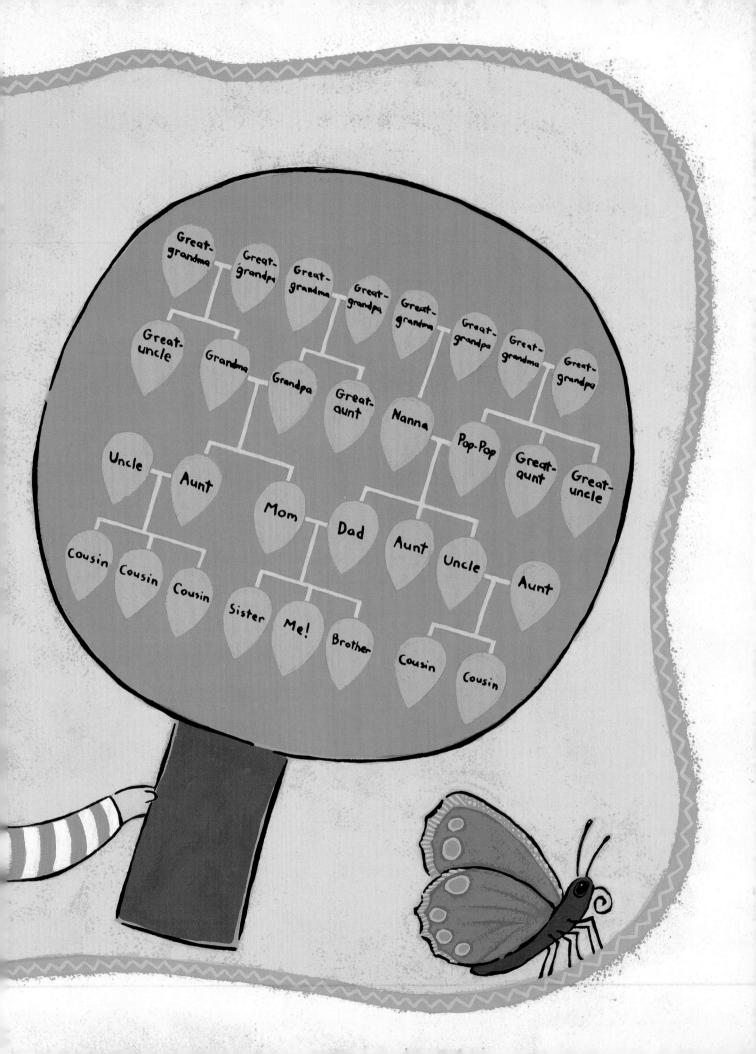

Who has finished making a family tree?

For every
member of
my family,
with love

Library of Congress Cataloging-in-Publication Data
Leedy, Loreen.
Who's who in my family / written and illustrated by Loreen Leedy.
—1st ed.
p.   cm.
ISBN 0-8234-1151-6
1. Family—Juvenile literature.   2. Kinship—Terminology—Juvenile
literature.   [1. Family.]   I. Title.
HQ744.L44   1995   94-16611   CIP   AC
306.85—dc20

Who's Who in My Family?

written and illustrated by
Loreen Leedy
Holiday House - New York

Out in open water, it wasn't so crowded, but there was still plenty to see. Several porpoises followed behind the *Loon,* and a dozen harbor seals were sunning themselves on a cluster of rocks just offshore.

At noon the wind dropped, and Mr. Johnson let the *Loon* drift toward a large island nearby. When it was close, he dropped anchor, and everyone climbed into the borrowed dinghy.

As they reached shore, Hillary and Suzanne helped pull the little boat onto the beach while Mrs. Johnson spread out a picnic lunch. After eating their sandwiches, Hillary and Suzanne went wading up to their knees in the ocean. The water was so cold it turned their skin pink and numbed their toes.

On the return trip, Hillary's dad let the girls ride in the dinghy as he towed it behind the *Loon*. They peered into the deep, black ocean until the sun, wind, and waves made them sleepy.

That evening, just as they tied up in Castine Harbor, there was a spectacular show of fireworks. From the Johnsons' mooring, Hillary and Suzanne felt as if they could almost touch the sparks. The glittering white fireworks were Hillary's favorite, while Suzanne liked the powerful BOOMS that shook her whole body.

At dawn, Hillary woke to a gentler sound: a low quack, quack, quack. It was the drake mallard, paddling among the boats, looking for food. Hillary's father had already rowed to the mainland and brought back their breakfast from the bakery. They had eaten long ago, and now the Johnsons were preparing to go home. Before they left, Hillary went to check on the nest one last time. Sure enough, right there in the bow of the rowboat, the hen mallard was patiently sitting on her eggs. When she finally stood up to preen, Hillary spied two more eggs, making ten altogether!

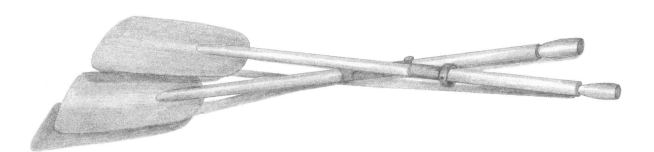

Although the Johnsons came to sail in Castine every week-end for the rest of the month, it wasn't until the very last day of July that the mallards eggs began to hatch. Luckily, Hillary and Suzanne were there to watch it happen. At first one egg began to tremble; then it shook—more and more—until it cracked. The crack grew bigger and bigger until, suddenly, a beak poked out! After that the shell split quickly, and there sat a new duckling. He was still wet from being inside the egg, but as the baby duck dried in the sun, his feathers became fluffy.

It took all day for the next six eggs to hatch. When the last duckling was dry and alert, the mother mallard led her troop to the water's edge. Before long, a wave rose up and floated all of them. Hillary and Suzanne laughed as the ducklings bobbed along behind their mother. They all looked exactly alike! It was quite a family.

With seven ducklings to care about, the month of August was a lot of fun. Hillary and Suzanne watched them closely and could even tell them apart by the way they behaved. Hillary was especially fond of the duckling that made lots of peeping noises. Suzanne's favorite was the one that was always hungry. Everyone at the boatyard asked the girls about their duckling friends. The local newspaper even sent a photographer to take a picture.

The hen mallard continued to take care of her brood, and they grew up quickly. But late in the summer, Suzanne noticed that the mother duck was sleeping more and more each day. The father duck—the drake—who had not helped in raising the little ones, was changing, too. His once colorful feathers had become dull brown.

Afraid that the mallards were sick, the girls decided to consult Suzanne's grandpop. But when she and Hillary described what was wrong, he only laughed. "Every year, at just about this time, a mallard's feathers fall out and are replaced by plain brown ones until their new feathers grow in. It's called 'molting' and helps camouflage the ducks while they rest on the shore."

"But why do they sleep so much?" asked Hillary.

"They're restin' until their new feathers grow in," said Grandpop. "And they're savin' energy for their migration south, when the weather turns cold."

In September, the Johnson family returned to the Eatons' boatyard for their last sail of the season. When they brought the *Loon* back to the shore, Suzanne's father helped Mr. and Mrs. Johnson pull her out of the water and secure the sloop for the winter.

The sun was setting earlier each day, and a cool wind often made the ocean choppy with whitecaps. Hillary and Suzanne noticed that the ducklings had grown real feathers in place of their soft down. The hen and drake mallard had new plumage, too. Knowing that the ducks would fly south any day now made the girls feel sad.

"Cheer up," said Grandpop. "They'll be back next year .... and, Hillary, so will you!"

The End